A Poet's Legacy On a Razor's Edge

Rod Keller

Published by A Less Traveled World Press, 2023.

A POET'S LEGACY ON A RAZOR'S EDGE

First edition. March 8, 2023.

ISBN: 979-8215605790

Written by Rod Keller.

Dedicated to my wife Ann

who has saved my life

more times

than I can count

or she would realize.

PREFACE

This is a book written based on my memory of events, places, people, and what they said. As such, it is fallible and only based on my best recollections of such events.

This book is a memoir of my *working life* as a minion, colleague, mentor and manager (sometimes all at once). My private life – the wonderful times and remembrances with my wife, as well as my immediate and extended family) will remain just that: private, protected and cherished within.

I begin my story in my teens, with a few recollections and events during my upbringing as key context regarding my world view and the roots of my sense of self.

As to the people and places and moments covered in my career days, I have written about a few (but not nearly all) of the key people with whom I worked. When I have mentioned people who are still living, I have also changed their names in order to keep them at peace, and me out of court. A few of my former colleagues are, unfortunately, not above ground any longer, and I have used their actual names in this book.

My descriptions of my professional life: people, places and situations is quite subjective. Places I have worked, and clients with whom I have worked are, in some case, noted. But not all. Situations are pinned down as accurately as I can recall them. Other participants and former colleagues might remember things differently. That's fair. Descriptions of past events and situations is quite subjective, and come through the often-faulty cameras of our memories.

Take Great Falls, Montana for instance. Their Chamber of Commerce currently would describe it as "a great place to live, raise a family and enjoy everything that Montana has to offer." This differs from my own image of Great Falls as a "drab, uninspiring, cold, barren place that is lacking in most things vital to having an enjoyable life."

It's all a matter of perspective, preferences and interpretation. And who knows, maybe Great Falls has improved over time.

So, if you disagree, just take it in stride. Maybe I am right; maybe I am wrong. I guarantee that my recollections will be different from yours.

FOREWARD AND ACKNOWLEDGEMENTS

A broken cable railing, a former CIA officer's mistake, the girl in the green dress: these are a few of the most significant totems of my life. All were mile markers of serendipity and possibility. Each changed my future and opened doors to adventure and transformation.

The tricky thing about life is that sometimes the ramifications of seemingly innocuous choices ripple out across time and circumstance. They create, in turn, cascades of unknowable and distantly significant results. And the things that hit you never seem to come from the direction from which you expect them.

In my own journey, when I had so earnestly hoped for certain things to occur, I sometimes did not recognize them for what they were. In a few cases, I nearly ignored those moments as they presented themselves. So, pay *really* close attention. Your very life may depend upon it.

You will find that I like to honor those who help and believe in others. So here, I want to acknowledge a few people who believed in me and made a world of difference:

Ann, the girl in the green dress who, the day after we first met, I swore I would marry. And did.

Fred, who gave me my first real job.

Mim, who hired me twice.

Daniel, a lifelong friend and one of the coolest people I have ever known.

Lana, who sponsored my Phoenix-like return to the big time.

And lastly the improbable Putney Westerfield, a smart and gentle man who mistook me for someone else. In doing so, he changed my life forever.

CHAPTER I: REALITY BITES

I thought I was done for. I had been hanging out with a sketchy friend at our normal Chicago street-corner when a police cruiser came by. Apparently when the police stopped the two of us, they detected something a bit off with me. Then, everything went to hell.

They shoved me into the back of the squad car, and started interrogating me about a botched hold-up by someone in our gang. A gun. And a murder. Some genius we knew had held up a popular streetside produce stand, then panicked and managed to shoot the store owner in the face. Dead.

What made this worse was that I was carrying a concealed weapon: a deadly dagger with an eight-inch blade hidden in the lining of my jacket.

Shit was getting real. And not at all going according to plan. Let me back up a bit and explain...

A POET'S LEGACY ON A RAZOR'S EDGE

I grew up in an apartment in Rogers Park, a neighborhood on the far north side of Chicago.

I was born to two well-meaning and highly creative people. While they were good humans and great parents, both came from broken homes, both had terrible role models as (often absentee) parents, and neither had a formal education. In sum, they had no fixed idea of what a parent should do or what they should teach to their children. Despite their very best motives, they were without sufficient training, background or experience to help me find my way in the world. With this circumstantially poor parental toolbox, it was indeed a wonder that they were able to ad lib and be any sort of parents at all! Nevertheless, they somehow figured it all out, and managed to offer us kids a pretty decent childhood in the end.

When I was a young boy, our family had very little money. My father, for most of his career, was self-employed. Just out of the Army, he started as a laborer at a machine shop. Then, he got a poorly rewarded hourly piece-rate job at an art studio. Back then artists got paid terrible wages. If he got work, he got paid. If not, there was no money. My mother occasionally took a few part time weekend jobs to help make ends meet, first as a part-time bank teller, and then later as the weekend receptionist at a small hospital in the suburbs. We struggled economically until I was about 18 years of age, when my mother got a series of more steady work in classified ad sales, proof reading and later in life, copy editing.

Most people may not fully realize the toll that having little money takes on a person, or a family. To comparatively have less money and be seen as "lesser than" one's peers, no matter the absolute amount, accumulates into a sort of personal weight that one carries around, sometimes for much of their lives. I say this so as to explain a significant aspect of my childhood.

Our parents did the very best they could to shield us from the economic inequities of our situation. But it was hard to disguise: for much of my youth we lived from payday to payday. With less food and less of just about everything than all our neighbors. We had one car, usually a jalopy of a machine that was in the process of breaking down so it could kill us. Mom would crisscross utility bills to keep the wolves from the door. There were no food stamps or food banks or other social programs during the 1950s. A household was more or less left to their own devices to get by as best they could.

With little money to spare, niceties were few and far between. Even buying one of us kids a candy bar had to be thought through in advance. The checkout girls at the local grocery hated seeing us on busy days. Unfortunately, we never had enough money to pay for the items in our cart, so mom always had me "take back" items once the clerk had totaled them. Then the poor clerk would have to manually recalculate the total. The other shoppers in line were always irritated at our holding up of the line, and our inability to pay the tab.

We all know about the social sides of middle-school and high school, and how vicious it can be. For me it was a little challenging: I wore the hand-me-downs from the two nerdy kids next door. I inherited their Sears-bought clothing starting at age five, and wore them through high school. I wore comically unfashionable and ill-fitting clothes that were at least five years out of date. Again, from Sears. Everything from underwear to pants and shoes and jackets were from this terrible fashion collection.

Meanwhile, my peers were from households where clothing and other conspicuous consumption totems signaled one's station in life. So, dressed in my weird out-of-date Sears couture, I had a bit of an uphill social battle and a very strong economic incentive to save up enough money to buy better clothes when I could.

A POET'S LEGACY ON A RAZOR'S EDGE

I started working part-time at a drug store at the age of 13, not because I was some hard-working kid, but because it was the only way to have any money at all. And to avoid wearing somebody else's used underwear.

Happily, my parents were both in the arts. My dad, a commercial artist, taught me a lot about creativity, the process of living, the predictability of the human race, about the natural world and about behavior (both human and otherwise). Dad was of Nordic descent, both soft and strong, tough as nails, taciturn and way deeper than most. He loved studying cultures, and wished he had been born a Native American for their beliefs and ways, if not their arts.

My mother, also an intellectual, was a poet first, and a writer/editor second. Occupationally she worked hard and ultimately became a copy editor with World Book Encyclopedia and then went on to become Assistant Editor for their Science Year periodical... She knew a lot about a lot. You never ever wanted to go against her in Trivial Pursuit. Mom was opinionated, intense, talkative, and mercurial at times. Not more than 5 feet tall, she grew up in Scotland, once lived on a boat, had been a champion swimmer in her youth, loved golden slippers and reminded me at times in both presence and intellect of a magical woodland elf.

Both of my parents were compelling as people and magnetic in their own ways: quick of the mind, opinionated, and well-read, they were continually inventive and loved silly fun. To my immense and unending happiness, in the last chapters of their lives, they applied their great skills by creating a series of about 15 wonderful children's books. This happily allowed them to dance and tarry in fields of metaphorical clover through their later years.

Dad was an incredibly creative presence in our young lives as kids. With little money, he somehow managed to create a wonderful collection of toys out of thin air, brick-a-brack, sticks and glue: including some life-defining kayaks made from pine and painted canvas, a wonderful replica soap box race car, a small sailboat, and even a kid-sized WWI (pretend) biplane. And that's just the short list. For all of this wonderful mirth and creativity surrounding us, we kids were lucky beyond measure. Despite being relatively penniless, we had a really happy time and some cool and unusual custom-made things. Among our friends, we were the hit of the neighborhood for all of dad's vivid inventions. The bi-plane even got us coverage in Popular Mechanics magazine.

Imagination was our special key to success. Imagination was the lead source of freedom in our young lives.

So was the beach. Given my mother's love of the water, we miraculously found a way to live near the beach on my parents' tiny budget. Our family's first apartment was only a block away from a beautiful sandy shore on Lake Michigan, and the second apartment was even closer! Of course, we kids lived every day we possibly could on that beach, weather be damned. For us a beach day was whenever we were not in school. (Yes, there might have been a few unexcused absences here or there.) Rocket fuel for our young imaginations, we kids liked to live on our beach year-round. It was our kingdom by the sea. So, while as a family we seemed to never have nearly enough money, the fairy-tale freedom of living along this beach washed the economic downsides away like sand in the surf. Recalling her own childhood by the North Sea, our mother had a sign that read, "If you're lucky enough to live by the sea, then you're lucky enough."

We always felt lucky enough, living on what seemed like the edge of the world.

A POET'S LEGACY ON A RAZOR'S EDGE

My formative years were an odd lot. I met my friend Mike after he almost shot me in the head with an arrow. Somebody who could shoot a bow and arrow just had to be my worst enemy or my best friend. And it was his odd-fellow spirit that tilted the table, making him my best friend. Then there was Dave, also from the next block over, who had previously lived in a rural ranch-y area, knew everything about horses (a rarity for a city kid), and wore actual cowboy boots. Dave was a smooth talker, handsome as a rock star, and a very handy guy to have around. Almost inseparable, we three musketeers did everything as a team, we even worked at the same street corner drugstore fountain together. We had a great time and loved to explore and pal around in our good-natured way.

We once got permission to take the train to Palatine, then a very far-away place, to visit Dave's old hometown. We'd go horseback riding, Dave promised. When we got to Palatine we visited Jose, one of Dave's old friends. After a few minutes there, his dad chastised him because Jose was supposed to be "taking care of the chickens." Being a city kid, I had a Disneyesque interpretation of that phrase, imagining that Jose would be feeding them, perhaps patting them on their little chicken heads.

But no. Jose's dad had asked him to "take care of them" as a mafia boss might have meant. In this case, "taking care of them" was all about breaking their necks, decapitating them, and then plucking them. Bam, bam, bam, bam. I can remember Jose walking back to the kitchen holding four plucked, bloody and extremely dead birds by their feet, two per hand.

We did go horseback riding, later that day. Funny thing: even though it was my first time on a horse (and almost got bucked off), that ride is not my most vivid memory of that day. Go figure.

The three of us had a lot of adventures and shared a lot of often not-so-safe situations as we grew up in Chicago. Through it all, we kept our humor, our cool (mostly), and (unlike those Palatine chickens) our heads. We soon discovered other kids like us a block over from that. And other kids. And even more kids.

Soon our garrulous and ever-growing group of teens, with the three of us at its rollicking, delinquent center, hung out routinely either at the beach or at the street corner drugstore fountain where Dave, Mike, and I all worked interchangeably as soda jerks, dishwashers, and delivery boys. It was, all told, a noisy, raucous, and totally grand time.

Coming of age in the late 60s and early 70s, I found myself firmly against the war in Viet Nam. This political stance was not at all the norm in our conservative and flag-waving neighborhood. I was quite used to being in the extreme minority and often chastised as a cultural outsider.

We did have a local counter-cultural spot, a head shop. While I hung out at the local head shop as a young teen, I did so more for the black light posters than the politics. Truth be told, I did not totally buy their thing, either. The drug references and paraphilia made me nervous: I had someone in my family who had an addiction to alcohol, and so I avoided drugs and alcohol until the middle of college, out of fear that this addictive tendency might be in me, too.

The point is that I did not fit any particular "type," and found that I had to really work at things in order to feel like I was a part of any crowd. Even though I had my few close friends, this outsider feeling was always there. Even as I adopted more of a socially liberal attitude, I did not fit that mold entirely, either. No single tribe or dogma seemed to fit me.

In those days, as today, there was much social discord. And in those times, everyone seemed to be testing everyone else, to see what they were all about. And in those times, I got called out for my inconsistencies, because I picked and chose my beliefs like I would pick at food at a salad bar. My "unpredictable" nature annoyed people because they could not guess my feelings or pin me down. Tough for them certainly. Odd for me, of course. While I often sided with people bold enough to violate the law and evade the draft, I did not ascribe to every one of their beliefs, either. Intellectually, following a well-trodden path would have been the easier path. This constant positional ambiguity was exhausting.

Since I never felt like I totally fit any one mold, I increasingly felt socially, politically, and even philosophically isolated; more of an island to myself. As a (now) 15 or so-year-old kid this was a bit intense. Even scary at times.

So here is the thing: looking at this rationally, I could see where things were headed for me. Not in any woo-woo sort of way, but more from a manner of plain old 15-year-old predictive logic. I was in this lower-class urban situation. Alone. I often saw the ills that were rampant in any city: addiction, drugs, and violence. With this as the environment, and not having much in the way of real knowledge or guidance on much of anything, I was becoming increasingly concerned that I was not going to make it long-term in this often ugly urban world.

It seemed dispassionately straightforward: There were simply so many things I was bewildered about which stood to harm people. And here I was in the middle of all this urban chaos, with no resources at all. I felt increasingly sure that I might not make it to middle age, I had a growing concern that something or other would do me in.

It was not a fear. It was a type of detached, resolved calculus that became more and more obvious as I got progressively closer to the dark maw of emerging adulthood. My parents, nice people, were pretty clueless themselves about adulthood. And because I had no guides, no back-up and no reliable weapons or demonstrable skills, I felt woefully unprepared. I felt like I was holding up a pen knife in the face of a fire-breathing dragon. Utterly and ridiculously unprepared.

This almost comic unpreparedness of mine: I felt like I was like playing a survival game in which there were no rules, no practice sessions, no preparation pointers, no boundaries—and in which I had no armor at all. It all just seemed damned steep of a hill. The future just seemed a bit, you know, unlikely. I eventually referred to all of this as the Early Demise Hypothesis.

THE SHATTERING OF THINGS

Time went on and our impromptu neighborhood "bunch" kept growing. Variously 10, to 20, to 30 strong at this point: we hung out in the colder months at the corner drug store where a few of us were semi-employed, and during the warmer months at the end of an iconic place along the Lake in Chicago called Farwell Pier.

Farwell Pier had an automated lighthouse of sorts at the end. It was picturesque and the subject of many photos in the area, sitting out there on Lake Michigan. Back in those days the beaches were smaller and the end of the pier was pretty far out in the lake. This gave the tip of the pier and its lighthouse a sort of windswept and secluded touch.

We three musketeers would regularly go out past the lighthouse at night to the very tip of the pier and sit on the lower cable railing, our feet dangling in space. There, we discussed life's important topics: cars, girls, music and the future. One evening in late October, with three of us sitting on the cables, the lower strand suddenly broke under our combined weight. Had we not been holding onto the top cable, we three would have been thrown into the deep, to face the daunting prospect of swimming back to the beach in that cold, black water.

The next afternoon was pretty stormy; typical for that time of year. The lighthouse, as usual in such weather, was constantly being hit violently by waves exploding as they hit the tip of the pier. We three friends used to dare one another to go out there in the wettest and windiest conditions. You had to hold on to the cables so as not to get blown off your feet. It was quite intense; not for the meek.

That wild afternoon, a neighborhood fellow who trained seeing eye dogs had made the questionable decision to go out to the end of the pier with his two German Shepherds. With the storm in full force, the tip of the pier was now getting hit with the full explosive fury of the lake. As he and the dogs went out past the lighthouse, a very large wave came up and pushed one of the dogs right through the hole we had made, into the surf. Seeing his dog in trouble, the neighborhood fellow then made another bad decision: he leaped in to save the dog.

He failed. Both disappeared.

Onlookers saw the surviving dog racing frantically back and forth on the pier, and along the shore to no avail, as its' master and mate were both lost in the water. Lifeguards, search and rescue boats, and the Chicago Police Department all joined the search. Nothing was found.

All that afternoon the beach and the water were crowded with would-be rescuers. Nothing. The storm continued into and through the night.

The next morning, with the weather still wet, windy, and drizzly, I walked the beach as I always did, today looking out at the angry waves... It was powerful weather: silt-gray, stormy, wet, and bone-cold. As I approached a segment of the beach piled with rocks and rip-rap, I came upon one of my best friends. Mike sat hooded and hunched close over a small bonfire he had built up very tight against the meager shelter of the rocks. With grim nods exchanged, I joined him.

The two of us huddled low, trying to stay dry, desperate for the warmth of the flames and any shelter the rocks could offer. After a bit, we talked in short sentences and halting tones, bent and hiding from the wind and deep damp, there in the colorless gloom of the rocks. We sat for a long time in miserable silence, just staring into the gray-on-gray blurred horizon of our little ocean. We shivered as much from the damp air as from the close breath of yesterday's death.

We both well knew our part in this terrible situation. A good guy died. His dog, it died. Both gone, we felt, because of something we had done; because of a break that we had caused in the cable. It was a bottomless pit of doom. Mike's family, like most in our working-class neighborhood, were staunch Irish-Catholics, and far more religious than mine. I knew this and imagined how he must feel, what he must be fearing. We were staring down death; staring down the devil. There was not much point in talking about it.

At the age of 15, neither of us had been in any sort of experience like this before. We felt afraid, guilty, unsure of what to do or say next. So, we just sat there together with our nervous anxieties, shivering into the endlessness of the gray spray, into what seemed like eternity. We shared this tense vulnerable moment, shivering and waiting... waiting... for something we did not understand. Maybe we were waiting for the hand of fate, or God, or the universe, or whatever else there was, to help us. Maybe we were hoping this might somehow even guide us at this precipitous moment in our pitiful, despicable, and vulnerable lives. Maybe. Waiting.

Then we both saw it at once: something in the waves. Just there, then gone. Then back again, in the surf. Something dark. It was twisting and tumbling closer in the waves, closer and higher as the water became shallower and as the waves worked on the dark mass. Our hopes and anxieties rose in tandem. We were not even sure what we were wanting to see. But in a moment, the mass tumbled, it was unmistakable: the hind leg of a dog. It was the lifeless body of the drowned dog.

In no time the police arrived, as neighbors must have also been keeping watch of the surf from their apartments lining the beach. People amassed. The body washed up. It was our lonely rocky coastline no more.

This was my first, devastating, horrible and unexpectedly intimate experience with death. A dog. But ... the death of a good being. A being that, had it lived, would have helped people. Tied to the death of a person who was trying to help people. A good and selfless person, we thought. A human death that, for a fact, we were directly tangled up in.

This was a moment without equal: personal, sorrowful, hollow, the darkest of dark blackness. It was a deep and endless plain of death and sadness. Final. Irrevocable and something that nobody should hold. But I had to own this. Looking at Mike's face, I saw that he too, felt it just as much, perhaps even more.

The terrible finality of death was right there in front of us on that lonely, wave swept and rocky shore. A shore that was, in reality, just a half block from home. And today, more than fifty years later, I can still see and feel every bit of that when I walk past those rocks.

Life went on; it had to. Eventually, the good man's body was found washing up on a beach several miles away.

Things evolved. Feelings washed clean. And in time the event was over-written by every other occurrence of every other moment of every new day.

A POET'S LEGACY ON A RAZOR'S EDGE

CHEESE IT

There is a thing about groups: at a certain point, group dynamics become a thing unto themselves. And when you are in such a group, it is like being caught up in a strong ocean current; you just go along, because you have little choice in the matter. I have witnessed this at parties, concerts, and gatherings. Sociologists point to this and how crowds develop emergent norms based on the norms not of society but of the crowd itself. Incrementally, extremist behaviors become more and more acceptable within the crowd. Gradually, such crowds become (sometimes violent) mobs, and can lose their way vis-à-vis regular societal norms and behaviors. As our collection of kids got bigger, it suddenly became this sort of "something else." These dynamics ruled the day.

Gradually, here and there, a few of the kids we hung out with in this large and vaguely tribal pack were getting into trouble. It started slowly. Then it escalated. And what was more alarming, the acceleration itself accelerated. From innocent lagging for quarters to a little graffiti. Then mean-spirited vandalism. Stealing property. Then, stealing cars.

At a point, the cops had given us a name; "North Shore Grease." Legitimacy, whether we wanted it or not. With a defined territory, other gangs didn't mess with us. Then we egged this on, we enforced this. Threats. Knives. Cudgels. There were rumbles. Three of them, specifically. On the beach at night. There were arrests and detentions in Juvenile Hall.

The escalation continued: one guy, a quite supreme idiot that hung around with us, decided to rob an open-air produce market. It was such a nice place, too; everyone went there. Then, apparently, (I think it was the first time he had tried something like this) he panicked during the hold-up. His gun went off, and he shot the owner in the face. He shot him dead.

In the weeks leading up to this event, I had turned 16 and my mother, who had not been back to Europe in over 20 years, brought me back to her hometown in Scotland. (What an adventure!) While there, I was presented with a family treasure: a (relatively worthless) ceremonial dagger from India which had a very sharp, fairly illegal, eight-inch blade. My great-uncle coached me on how to smuggle it into the US upon my return—which I may or may not have done.

When I did return to the US, I had somehow or other re-acquired the dagger. Being a 16-year-old boy, I had no idea it was a worthless knock off, so my very first instinct was to show this very cool thing off to my friends on the street corner where everyone hung out.

Having recently come back into the States, I had absolutely no knowledge of the hold-up, the murder, or the possibility that the police might be interested in talking to us. But, lucky me. They came, and right at that moment I had this quite illegal and extremely deadly dagger right there, in my possession.

I remember the moment when the police cruiser pulled up: I was sitting astride the top of a mailbox, as though on a horse. I had moments earlier been told of the botched hold-up and murder, and so had stashed my dagger in a (not very) "secret" pocket inside my jacket. So, when the police car stopped and the patrolmen got out, I added up the issues.

Police. Suspicion. Murder. An illegal demon-killer dagger in my pocket. And one last thing: terrible timing. That's about when the adrenalin kicked in. I felt like puking my guts out.

Now, I have a pretty strong stomach. But... when I have that green-tinged "cookie hurl" look about me, it's kind of hard to hide. And, just guessing here, but I think it was that distinctive green-toned look which our keen-eyed patrolmen must have noticed, and made him beckon me saying, "Come over here, kid!"

Boy, I am glad I did not lose it at that moment. A "green-toned-shoes" incident would have been bad for us both, for sure. But, on the other hand, maybe it would have distracted the cops from the knife, so there's that.

Anyway, they questioned us both: first outside and then inside the police car. Very luckily, they did not pat me down to find my lost-world dagger. Had it been discovered, my prized possession would have at least landed me in Juvie, and likely resulted in some sort of criminal record.

In the end, I kept my dagger and my cookies. I got a free (queasy) ride home in the back of their squad car. Of course, (curse my luck) my dad watched us pull up to our apartment building. That did not go so well. It was the only time my dad ever struck me. And he did not even know the dagger part of the story. All told, I deserved that slap for stupidity alone, and never held it against him at all.

Once just a few friends hung out at a corner soda fountain, and now things were evolving too fast, to a terrible end. Everything had spun crazily out of control. I had inadvertently come really close to the edge, and knew it. We were a gang now. And an innocent guy was shot dead. The police. Shit was now so very real.

This caused a full stop moment in my head. Everything looked perfectly laid out, as though I was watching from a distant ledge. I saw it all. I absolutely knew what I had to do: I had to make a very major and deliberate change.

While many of these guys were good friends and I regretted leaving this core group, I saw this path. It went in a direction that I saw laid bare, for all its perils. Here I was; I was resolved. I made the very conscious decision to leave this all behind. My friends, my job, my habits. All, entirely. All at once. Right now. I promised myself that I would never look back.

I left.

It was a hard but important choice. After making that decision, I will admit that life was pretty tough. Lonely. I second-guessed my decision several times. It hurt.

In time, I found a few new friends at school, and a new routine that revolved around innocuous things like revolving poker games and going out for pizza. To be honest, this new group and rhythm all seemed boring in comparison to the crowd I had been hanging with on the street corner. But then again, after all that drama and danger in my former life, "boring" seemed a better alternative than where the other path led.

It was not without issue: one or two of the people in this group were a bit annoying, but I could not very well pick and choose. It was a package deal. These guys, unlike my old crowd, had much more affluent parents, came from stable homes, would never be arrested, would quite likely all get into college, and they'd probably all live in the suburbs one day. Have careers. Stability. Could I see myself on that path? Well, not really. But again, it was the better alternative.

So, while it was hard at times to stay the course, I kept to my promise to myself and never once went back to the old gang. I never visited the old haunts; I never again hung with any of the old crowd. I got a new job at a grocery store I had never even visited, in a different part of town. I got it on the referral of one of these new friends. In a while the new crowd became my crowd, and I came of age with this new poker and pizza group during the late 60s and early 70s.

I found a new life. And while it did not totally fit me, I successfully transitioned away from that gang of greasers.

THE WAR MACHINE

The Viet Nam war had been going on for quite some time, mostly in the background of our lives. As the soldiers on the evening news looked more and more like guys our age, it became much more real to us all. More and more grave, too.

There was a lottery for the draft, and on every male's 18th birthday he became eligible. Each birth date got a number, from 1 to 365. And when your age group was called, you were asked to report for your armed forces physical exam. They started with "1" and then called up higher and higher, depending on how many soldiers they needed for the war machine. So, the higher your (randomly drawn) number was, the safer you were from not being called. My number was in the mid-90s, and near the cut-off but relatively high. At first, I was comfortable with the likelihood that I would not be called in to report for my physical exam (the first step in the induction process). But as the war crept on, the war machine needed more men, more soldiers for the war machine, more bodies. And the selective service kept calling up more and more guys. And agonizingly slowly, like a rising sea tide, the calls came closer and closer to my number.

One morning I was standing at the elevated train station, commuting into the city to my day job and later, to my night school. I spied my old best friend Dave's former girlfriend Lori (from the old gang).

"Did you hear about Dave?" she had a concerned look on her face like something terrible had happened. "Dave got called in to take his physical." It was pretty terrible. But it wasn't just Dave.

As Lori knew, Dave and I shared the same birthdate, and the same draft number. Our number was up. Literally. I got the same selective service notice to report for my physical exam later that day.

I had no deferment. I had no conditions that would keep me from being drafted and sent to Viet Nam. This was it.

Politically, I was dead set against the war in Viet Nam, feeling that it was not any of our business. More importantly, the reader will note that I also had this very personal experience about life and death on the beach. Death, to me, seemed a terrible and almost inexcusable thing to inflict on another random person just by the pull of a trigger. And I'd never walk that back.

Given my deep conviction about not wanting to kill anybody at all, I applied for Conscientious Objector (CO) status. My task was not easy: I had to convince a board of 12 flag-waving, football-loving, and manly men that my deeply held beliefs prohibited me from killing anyone. It seemed a mighty daunting mission. I strongly felt this was morally wrong.

Usually, people who were given CO status came from very religious backgrounds, and or had recommendations from clergy, or others. With this, it was still quite a steep hill: only some were granted CO status, usually as a direct result of holding dear that life situation and belief system.

I, on the other hand, had a big basket full of problems: I was not a member of any organized religion. Worse, I was a Sunday School drop-out. I had once told the Sunday School teachers that I thought the whole thing with bushes that could talk was "stupid," and created a scene at the time. The Sunday School teachers actually stopped the class and had my parents take me home on the spot.

After that, I had hardly ever in my entire life even set foot in a church. I had made no secret of the fact that I was pretty leery of organized religion: it all seemed too rich and powerful, and I was convinced it had been responsible for some terrible things all through history. But all this notwithstanding, I had my beliefs. And I did not see any conflict between my beliefs and my view of religion as an occasionally evil institution. My world views all seemed congruent and logical to me. And being an idealistic and too-full-of-himself idiot, I was not about to lie about any of my feelings about organized religion, even if it caused me problems.

In other words, this situation was what you might call "rife with difficulty."

To my (begrudging) amazement, there was a group that helped people – even people like me: the Quaker Friends Organization. I hung on them for advice like it was a life raft. They helped me craft my written submission. I was open about my feelings about organized religion, but they helped me out of a sense of a larger mission. It was humbling, and made me believe there was goodness in the world after all.

With the kind guidance of the Quakers, I submitted my written statement to the board about my actual story of the stormy night on the pier, and the good man, and the dog. I mentioned my feelings: the profound emptiness, the dread, the horrible finality... all of it, in writing to the draft board. This was my experience, the one that cemented my intense beliefs about death, dying and culpability, regret and ethics. But I was not Catholic, or Protestant, or Buddhist, or anything. Pessimism and cynicism – those were my religions.

I did not think I had a chance in hell of getting through this with a favorable outcome. I realistically contemplated the two most likely next moves: either going to Viet Nam or leaving for Canada to live with my uncle. Either choice would have changed my life forever. Damned Early Demise Hypothesis!

Then, one morning a letter came in the mail from the Selective Service. I dreaded this. Most likely it would be terrible news. The end result would be plane ticket either to Southeast Asia or Toronto. And who knows if I would ever come back. This seemed like a pretty crappy ending, either way.

I waited until my parents were both home until I opened it. To our great astonishment and my eternal relief, the 12-man board tentatively granted my Conscientious Objector status. I read and re-read. Over and over. Tentatively. It was a tentative approval. The final decision would be made after an upcoming personal appearance before the board. While not at all final, it was encouraging. Fate was not done with me quite yet.

An introvert, I sweated over the impending personal appearance. A perpetually bewildered and generally insecure guy at this early point in my life, I was sure I would just melt in front of a review board. "What if a Communist killed your sister?" Famously, that was the sort of questions that they leveled at people in these board hearings. I had no idea of the "right" answer to those types of questions. Or if there ever was a good answer to that sort of question. I very deeply dreaded this upcoming hearing.

But this was my fate; I had no choice. I must wait it out, and then go and stand in front of this group of manly men. I was certain they would see me as a pitiful and cowardly communist sympathizer. That's what most opinion leaders said about "people like me." I mean, the majority of people felt that scum like me should all stop whining, man up, salute the flag and go off to war. The broad societal pressure of conformity was ever-present, extremely oppressive and an ongoing condition of life right now. And who knows, maybe they were right? Maybe I was wrong?

Then something unimaginable and almost miraculous occurred: the peace talks in Paris, which had been going on for what seemed like a billion years, had actually gotten traction. The parties all agreed on terms! Then, the war was officially declared over. Really over. Fully and completely over.

But the fate of the selective service and the draft lottery? This bit was frustratingly unclear... still up in the air. My mother and I nervously called everyone we could think of for advice and counsel (no internet at the time, so facts were hard to come by). Then, the announcement came: The Selective Service was ceasing all operation (including draft board hearings), just a mere week before I was to appear before them! It was that close, that delicious, and that surreal. I was spared.

There are absolute and clearly seismic moments in one's life where a person is just plain dumbstruck, no matter how ignorant or smart, aware or unaware we are, no matter how introspective or oblivious. And in that one moment, standing there in my family's living room, with my parents and me all crying with relief, things just suddenly became incredibly and immediately obvious: my whole world had just changed. Profoundly. My very existence had just been altered in a permanent and significant way. From here on everything would be new: a brand-new future was being rewritten, starting right now, at this moment.

Once I had been staring into a deep dark hole in the Universe, and here I was: with the sudden realization that I get to Live. Escape. Be free. What I thought was going to surely be the end of me, was simply and permanently Gone.

What a long shot. What a huge break. Me: this dark horse of a fellow with a self-calculated short life expectancy now had a new door open. A supernatural door.

But life is not some TV show. There is no theme music, or credits, or end slate. No crane shot. So, at this point, life being what it is, absolutely nothing remarkable happened... the seconds just ticked by as they always had, and life went on, and things came and went like they always do. Just more seconds, minutes, and hours in the day.

Now, life went on... but with this glow of a difference: I was still Here. After all this crazy crap, I survived.

A lot of people believe in God; they believe in "manifesting" crap (whatever that means), they believe with all their being and intensity that prayer will help alter their fate; they believe that if they lead a good life (whatever that is), they will get good cosmic breaks in return.

But the thing of it is, I just do not think there is any such thing as a cosmic return. Bad people die. Good people die. Sometimes there are just terrible and awful turns of luck. A person can be in the middle of the most wonderful stage of life and get hit by a bus. Or fall into a grain auger. And die. Or not die, but instead be sentenced to living with whatever fate has befallen them.

Chances spin on a razor's edge. When we are spared and are viscerally aware we have just been spared, we are caught in a moment where lines of the world seem to converge, as we breathlessly wonder what might have happened if this or that was just a half-degree off. These are the inflection points of our very existence. Just a sliver of a degree, there is, between hope, glory, liberty or imprisonment. Life and death.

At this very particular inflection point of my life, still mysteriously chained by the Universe to the deaths on our beach some years past, I just stood there amped up on adrenaline, aware of my beating heart and the salt of my tears.

And it occurred to me that maybe the Early Demise Hypothesis was wrong.

A POET'S LEGACY

My mother the poet had penned this on the occasion of my birth:

It's a poet's legacy that I leave you then,

a lack of money and a love of men.

This passage in a poem, more than anything else, summed up my childhood for me.

While my extremely thoughtful and diligent parents gradually climbed out of their hand-to-mouth economic situation in time to make a more complete and more comfortable youth for my younger siblings, my own early childhood had been one in which we had little money for anything beyond life's necessities. Toys were a tough reach. Money for extracurricular things like restaurants, treats, camps, field trips... a very far and distant shore. Those were the things that 'rich kids' did or got, and just were not in the cards for a kid like me.

New clothes were an object of unreachable fantasy for most of my youth. I got pretty tired of wearing the ugly Sears hand-me-downs from our weird-kid neighbors. My awkward appearance made all social things pretty daunting, and was a convenient avenue for people to label me as odd. My coats were too big. My pants were way too short or too long and I would have to cuff them myself with pins. As time went on, I had part-time jobs and learned to adapt to my odd situation: I would alter my own clothes to make them fit better. At a point I taught myself how to sew in order to keep from getting stuck with the pins all the time. My shirts were too tight and the sleeves were too short, so I always hid that by rolling my sleeves up.

For some reason I never had short sleeve shirts, even in Summer. And somebody started the rumor that my arms were scarred because I was a heroin addict and the longer sleeves hid my track marks.

Socially, my life was a bit of crap. First, they called me geeky, and I was teased by some. I had to develop a tough exterior to combat this. And then later (as I became a part of the streetcorner gang and someone not to mess with) they labeled me as wild and dangerous. I was not bullied, but I was cast as unpopular, and was socially shunned. When I found things that actually fit well, I wore those articles of clothing all the time. Some photos of the period showed me in exactly the same long pants and shirt. Those were my good-fitting clothes, and so I wore them always.

But even through this ongoing weird social thing at school, I had made the transition to the pizza/poker crowd. For about two years, I was in this "between two worlds" sort of existence, since after all, kids talk. Nobody was really sure of who I was, or where I had come from. Just that I was "wild." I had a vague look about me that made some of these bully types a little uneasy. Probably due to my earlier streetcorner experiences, and because of what I had done and seen in my days with that crowd, I was not even the tiniest bit afraid of any of these bully-boy jokers. I suppose that my lack of fear was pretty obvious to them, which just made me seem a little bit "wilder."

There was one kid, Lennox, who had as his pastime, the hobby of bullying one of the fellows in my newly-adopted poker and pizza crowd. Like the gang I had been a part of before, I felt that there was a code: I felt honor-bound to aid anyone in this new poker/pizza group, even if I did not like them that much.

On this one particular early fall day in Sophomore year, as about 30 or 40 of us were all waiting amassed at the school entryway to get back into the air conditioning and out of the heat, Lennox started in on this poker/pizza group friend of mine, threatening to punch him.

Feeling my duty to come to his aid, I slipped in between them. "Hey Lennox, don't punch him, punch me!" I said loud enough for everyone to hear. "Punch me, right here, Lennox" indicating my chin, adding, "if you have the nerve."

Lennox paused, quite surprised at this turn of events and even more: quite unsure of what to do next. Then having no other option, he threw a punch, but with a lot less commitment than was necessary. I was moderately good at this sort of situation in those days, so I instinctively pulled back and to the left a little, with the result of Lennox's right fist merely glancing off my cheek. My turn: I swung hard with an upper cut and hit him in the midsection. Recoiling at the pain, he fell off the slightly raised platform, backward and into the grass and bushes. All he really had was a bruised ego, but the fight was over.

Fight over, friend rescued. Lennox silenced. And, I will also add this: from then on nobody ever said a single thing about my clothes, weird or otherwise.

Now with a "good" job as a produce clerk at a major grocery retailer, I had money in my pocket on a semi-regular basis. I vividly remember buying my first pair of blue jeans in that next year, at age seventeen. Blue jeans were in, and since the geeks next door never owned any, I never did either. I had saved money from my part-time jobs at the corner drug store and desperately wanted a pair of blue jeans. I had never been into a clothing store, at least that I could remember in my seventeen years. I had no more a clue as to how to go about this process as would a squirrel. While my mom must have taken me to one at some point in my early childhood, those memories were so long ago that I had zero memory of ever having done anything like this before.

So, one of my friends took me to the store. It was in the suburbs, and I could take you to that very address today. I did not let on at all to anyone, but this was a moment of extreme anxiety and trauma. I was wildly nervous and very self-conscious: I had absolutely no idea what to do or say, or how to act in this store. I had to just be mellow, stay alert to subtle cues, and absolutely not give myself away at any price. I was tremendously ashamed and embarrassed about my total ignorance, born from poverty, of what to do at a clothing store.

We walked in and my friend, being helpful and seeing me scan the place over and over, asked me my size. I had no idea. So, I started picking pants up and holding them to my waistline and looking down to see if they were long enough. That seemed logical. But my unfamiliarity with any of this became embarrassingly obvious. My friend diplomatically suggested that I take these pants to the changing rooms to try them on to see if they fit. I flashed a brief "really?" and then went along with this, in a combination of slight disbelief and with a little bit of disgust. It seemed gross to me that people would try on pants and then try on other pants and that if you bought pants, *someone else might have wearing them earlier that day*. But I soon saw that this was really the only way to make sure things fit well. Of course, getting a good fit was a relatively new concept to me. But I did it through trial and error, and successfully bought my first pair of blue jeans. It was all I could do not to wear them home!

In a nutshell, this was my reality, growing up. While some kids talk about being late bloomers, this took on a whole new dimension for me: a late bloomer in pants!

After going to the blue jeans store, (I was living the dream now, for sure) we went to a small record store and listened to a new record: Tea for the Tillerman by this new guy named Cat Stevens. Of course, being a teen, I had a few records, but I bought them curbside, at a huge discount, and mostly out of a car trunk. So, to be clear: I never had been to a record store. Never had the cash. The fact that you could listen to an album right there, and listen on *headphones* just blew my mind. Right there, I tried headphones for the very first time. What a day! My favorite cut was called "Miles from Nowhere." It had a great lyric about climbing a mountain. I had never seen a mountain. But with this day and its firsts, I felt the very moon was in reach. So, I sure had "seeing a mountain" in my sights!

Most of the poker and pizza kids I hung out with these days were Jewish, and several lived in free-standing houses. Some of their houses even had second stories on them: seemed like palaces to me. And yes, their parents often owned their own shops. Shopkeepers: this is what passed for "rich" in my world. The reality, of course, is that they owned modest businesses: pawn shops, second-hand stores, bail bond places. Not the best, but "been down so long, it seems like up to me," they had much more money than my family did. They bought their kids cars, paid for them to take European vacations, fashionable clothes... little materialistic things, sure; but worlds more than my family ever had.

I wanted more in life. More out of life. But I was clueless as to *what* that was, *where* I would find it, or *how* I – a long haired, leaping gnome of a person – would ever get there in my likely brief life.

A POET'S LEGACY ON A RAZOR'S EDGE

CHAPTER II: CARDINAL DIRECTIONS

After getting through the draft and the Viet Nam war years, life proceeded as life does. People came and went. Friends came and went. And after having drifted in and out of things that held my interest and attention for a time here and there, I finally found a thing, a focus, a topic... something that fascinated me endlessly. And thankfully, something that people pay money for... it was, in actuality, an honest to God career path.

I graduated with a social-psych degree from an average State school in the Midwest. Oh, I had gone through a few schools... first, Kendall College, a place that I referred to as "the broom closet of Northwestern" for its proximity to that school. It was in truth a community college for people with a much more money than good grades or solid study skills. Finding that school to be terrible, I went to an interesting and unusual school called Columbia College. Columbia was much more respectable than Kendall, but in those days just barely accredited. It was a communications college full of really innovative thinkers, housed in what honestly was a pretty decrepit building (the kind where you might rather not take the elevator) along Lake Shore Drive at the foot of Navy Pier. I ate at Navy Pier regularly... but when Navy Pier was an actual, brine-scented, working ship's pier and not at all a tourist trap. My dinner choice was a bona fide, working man's shrimp shack called Rocky's, on the very edge of the Lake Michigan's shore (still my home).

By day during this time, I worked for a long defunct place called Audio-Graphic films. We specialized in assembling 16mm industrial film cartridges that you used to see at trade shows or car dealerships. It was located in a forgotten low rent store front that might have once been a restaurant or book store or something. My job was to put a protective coating on the film and then load it into cartridges, which basically consisted of making make old-school splices and edits to the physical film in pre-selected places. It was a full-time job and paid a decent wage.

By night I went to school. I went about two years in this manner, and was majoring in film. I had been inspired by a documentary film maker friend of my parents. I found film-making really interesting, complicated, creative and fun. I wanted to edit, or direct or even write screenplays... something like that. As I tried my hand at editing at Columbia, I was unfortunately partnered with an actual, for real, habit-wearing nun. Just my luck.

We parted due to unreconcilable creative differences (go figure). Downtrodden, and wanting real editing experience I found out about a catch 22 in the Chicago film industry: you couldn't get a real job unless you were in the union, and you couldn't get into the union without a real job. Of course, that wasn't literally true, but that's what I had heard in no uncertain terms from some union guys. Hamstrung and about 20 years old at most, I felt thwarted. This and a few other atmospherics conspired to suppress my desire to perhaps find another lifepath. While my time at Columbia seemed like it was "wasted time," in the end this stint at Columbia would later prove to be pivotal in my life, enabling me yet another spin on the razor's edge. But that will have to wait for another chapter.

Despairing on this dead end, I decided to transfer to Northern Illinois University in Dekalb Illinois in my (second) Junior year. Here, I focused on the social sciences: anthropology, sociology and psychology. While I had heard that a few of the professors were extremely tough, I thought I must have heard it wrong because it all seemed ridiculously easy and very interesting.

In one experimental psych lab, we were tasked to input data into a computer and determine generally how the computer's algorithms were massaging the data by looking at the outputs. Each algorithm was replicating the optic nerve properties of different animals. I realized (to my total wonder and significant puzzlement) that I could actually do this very easily. I did it intuitively, consistently, and faster than anyone else in my class. At first, I shucked it to beginner's luck. And then I did it again, and again.

"How are you doing this?", asked my skeptical lab partners. I had no idea. I felt like they suspected me of having cheat notes or something. We replicated it over and over. The thing is, I kept sensing the right answer in sort of a holistic way, and hadn't the foggiest idea how I did it. It felt like magic. I would somehow "know" the solution and then work out the algorithm backwards. I was not a mathematics genius. To the contrary, I thought math was dreary and tedious. But I could do this intuitively, for some reason. It was a puzzle.

I remember all of this so brightly and vividly – the room, my lab partners, and the grad assistant with us at the time – because it was the absolute very first time that I ever considered that I might not be a bumbling idiot. I had no idea how I was doing this, but I actually *was* doing this. In an almost detached self-discovery moment, it made me smile in a sincerely surprised, "well I'll be damned!" sort of way.

Mind you, my Early Demise Hypothesis had been in part predicated on the fact that I actually *was* an idiot. Or generously, just not very smart. The logic was, I thought, unassailable: due to my at least marginally dullard tendencies, I would of course repeatedly make poor life choices. This in turn, would repeatedly put me into terrible predicaments. Eventually (the law of large numbers being what it is) one of these terrible predicaments would catch up to me and prove to be my undoing. Seems simple. Not cheery, but pretty obvious math, right? Natural consequences.

Then if that life calculus was not enough, there were complicating environmental and cultural matters. While I often (but not always) had close relationships with one or two people at a time, I never felt like part of a tribe or a larger collective. I was never much of a "belonger" to groups. And especially in urban environments, there is bona-fide survival value in being a part of a protective tribe, right? I mean, this all made so much sense. Again, just math.

So here was my dilemma: with this new and surprising evidence that *I may not be a complete idiot*—well it really screwed with the Early Demise Hypothesis. Messed it up in a huge way, in fact. I would clearly need to recalibrate my assumptions.

This science-and-psychology subject matter seemed incredibly interesting to me. I soon found myself leaning into it in a natural and excited manner. This became the focus of my deliberate second Junior year in college. Earlier, thanks to my dad, I had realized I had a general fascination with all sorts of behavior (animal, human, whatever), had an ease with anthropology, sociology and psychology and then – surprisingly give my long-held distain for math – I actually liked technology and science-based things like experimental design and survey research. So, here at the State run university, I gave statistics the benefit of the doubt, and to my added surprise, decided to then dedicate my studies to this nascent field of marketing research. It was all like walking past a mirror in a hat that somebody gave you, catching yourself by surprise in that reflection and realizing, "Hey, what do you know... not bad, not bad at all."

Finding this thing that I now delightedly and willfully obsessed over, I did quite well academically. Having once upon a time been a straight "D" student, my brain had been positively ignited. And here, I graduated with a respectably high GPA and a Bachelor's degree from an actual legit University. Adding to my feeling of victory, I was the first in my immediate family to get beyond a high school education.

Armed with a bachelor's degree in social-psychology in 1975, I moved back to Chicago to try and find a job in this relatively nascent field called marketing research. My graduation gift from my parents was an SR-10 Texas Instruments Calculator, also known at the time as a "pocket slide rule." It was cutting edge technology and my pride and joy. It is somewhere out there and still has my name on it.

NOW YOU ARE ONE OF US

While information was hard to come by in the days before the internet, I knew there was a large firm called Market Facts in Chicago that was active in this the field of marketing research. With this slender bit of information, I watched the Chicago newspapers for help-wanted ads from this particular company with the hyper-vigilance of a hungry hawk.

Finally, in mid-Summer of 1975 my moment came: I answered an ad they posted for something called a "coder," with not even the foggiest notion of what that was. I only knew that this was my one chance: if I got in the door there, I might be able to go even further.

Yes! I got the job. It had a low bar to entry (perhaps basic sentience). It was menial, at best. My job was mind-numbingly repetitive and consisted of looking at written responses to questions about the federal school lunch program. What did you eat today? I would read the answer and "code" or classify the answers according to pre-determined categories of responses. Aggregated, this became data that was then crunched, analyzed and reported by others. (Based on my early reads of this data, the world in those days seemed to run on hot dogs and apple sauce.)

The entire coding department – 28 people in total – sat in a silent, mildly dirty, white, featureless and windowless room that measured about 30 x 40 feet. The white walls were unadorned. These walls were interrupted only by three generic off-white metal doors.

The metal door at the front center of the room had a little window. If you peered into it while passing by, you could see a series of perhaps ten mainframe computers (each as big as a refrigerator), where serious-looking men in white short-sleeved shirts did mysterious things with reels of tape. Once, there was much shouting. The window shook. Nobody ever explained why. To my knowledge, nobody ever actually entered or exited through that door.

A second door, rarely used, was in the rear at the right. The VP in charge of data processing had an office that bordered the hallway somewhere in that direction. That's all we knew. We were not welcome to use that door.

There was another door at the far left at the front of our world. This was the door through which we coders came and went. It was a windowless door that led through a back linoleum-floored corridor past copiers and a punch card machine, to the elevators. Coders, it was made clear, were not allowed to go past the elevators or even approach the reception desk and lobby which could be seen through the double glass doors on the other side of the elevators.

Beyond the lobby and reception desk there seemed to be another world entirely. We could see that world, but were not allowed to go there. Past the nice marble-floored reception lounge, there was a palm-treed and decorated realm where clients came for meetings. It was a place where suited executives had offices, where people walked with urgency and focus, and where art hung on the walls in the carpeted hallways.

In our coder world, there were two types of metal desks. All were battleship gray in color. The smaller gray metal coder desks were arranged in three rows, six desks across, in pairs. The outside pairs of coder desks on the left and right were up against the walls, leaving a center row of desks and two rows between the pairs of desks, in which people might walk from the back to the front of the room. Our coder desks all faced the front of the room toward the door with the window, while our supervisors sat in the back, behind us and facing us. The only thing on that front wall other than the windowed computer room door was an industrial-looking clock. It ticked with each second-hand movement.

It was a quiet place, other than the tick-tick-tick of the clock and the occasional shuffling of paper.

We had rules. As coders we were prohibited from getting up, from talking, from eating, or even drinking anything but water at our workstations, lest it spill on our questionnaires. We were not to get up other than for (1) lunch or (2) bathroom breaks per day. All things were brought to us. Red pencils, questionnaires, a stapler. You kept all materials not being used in your drawer. There was no lunch room or break room. There was no refrigerator. You could keep a purse or a lunch box in your desk file drawer, but those personal items had to be gone at the end of your shift. That is all you kept in your drawer. This, it was patronizingly explained to us when we started and then repeated whenever there had been an "incident" (of non-compliance), was the only way in which things would work, given the small and constrictive size of our work area. I felt like a pig in a cage.

Our coding supervisor would bring us questionnaires and stack them on the right. We would process the open-ended responses, codify them and place the completes in a stack on the left. When ready for more uncoded questionnaires, we would raise our hands, at which point our coding supervisor would bring us new questionnaires (on the right) and take away the completes (on the left). *This* was the process. *This* was how it was done. *This* was the day. *This* would go on all day, every day. Week after week. For as long as you lasted at this job.

The clock ticked. The fluorescent lights hummed. We coded in silence, like monks with red pencils. All you could hear was the shuffling of questionnaires. It was a recipe for insanity. It was as oppressive as a George Tooker painting depicting an Orwellian situation: Inhuman, plodding, anonymous monotonous, gelatinous, deep and dark.

Behind us... right there ... right behind our backs, staring at us, sat our coding supervisors. Intimidating. Brooding. Whispering. They shuffled. We could not see them but we sensed them; heard them. And they were always there: just staring at us, making sure we were working. Not talking. Just there, behind our backs. All day. *This* was how it was done. *This* was the day. *This* would go on all day, every day. Week after week. For as long as you lasted at this job.

There were four supervisors back there, each in charge of six coders. They sat, each watching and monitoring their respective teams of coders stationed like horses or sled dogs, directly in front of them. The supervisors, all women in their mid-50s, had larger gray desks, appropriate to their higher elevated station in life. Our supervisor was named Candace. She, like the others, never smiled. It seemed to me perhaps an unspoken policy.

I was slightly ashamed of this job. I'd tell some friends about it in detail, and see the astonished looks on their faces. "I must get out of this hell as soon as possible," I would tell my friends. Then I'd go back to plotting my escape.

Being a psych major, out of sheer long-standing habit I tried to figure out Supervisor Candace. I developed this story: Candace was one of those people who had experienced a largely disappointing and mostly solitary life. This, I reasoned, had gradually made her bitter and resentful of anyone, but especially people who had more positive lives than she. A low bar. Look: by comparison my life was not all that wonderful. I was living with my parents, had very little money and had a pretty crappy job. But still, my life was perhaps a damn sight better than hers. So, I reasoned, it was perfectly logical that she hated me, too.

This is how my mind worked. I did not have a high need to be liked, but I did have a high need to figure everything out. And as long as I could find the logic in something, I could make peace with it, for what that's worth. And in this case, I could rationalize why people like Candace might hate me, and people like me.

Then one day I had a major breakthrough: I had to ask Candace a question that needed immediate response. So, on this one particular day I broke the rules and physically approached her desk. It seemed weird: I had never been back in the rear of this room before. Ever. At her desk was a DIY word-of-the-day device she had made for herself. The word of the day, written in her hand, was "despise." Seriously. "Despise." That cemented it, she must have had an equal-opportunity hate thing going on: She simply hated everybody.

EXECUTIVE PANTS

While the coding department's Orwellian hell was something to be endured, at least I had a great seat: front row, near the door and on the aisle, where the analytic people would walk back and forth from the entrance door to the desks of our lovely supervisors. I would try, usually in vain, to catch the eye of one or another; it was hard to do. But this high viz spot soon proved advantageous in my plan to escape this energy-sink of a room.

Joyce, my perpetually peppy coding buddy and confidant, sat to my right. A good-natured person and occasional lunch companion, if she needed to leave her desk for any purpose, our tight quarters required me to get up from my desk to let her pass. Sitting up tight behind me (leaving me just enough room to squeeze into my chair) was William. A small and mousy guy about age 30 or so, he lived with his mother. At one point we learned that she helped him with his digestive problems by regularly giving him something called "enemas." In my 20 some years on earth, I had zero occasions or anything like opportunity to know what an enema was. And while I generally knew the region in which an enema was done, I had to go to a bookstore in order to indulge my curiosity about what it might be. Ugh. So much for curiosity and cats. I wish I could have unlearned this bit. At least this explained the occasional odd odor wafting from someplace behind me. This information 100% validated my sense that he was an extremely creepy individual. I was quite confused at all this and tried my best to just not think too much about it at all. But it reignited my drive to get the hell out of there as fast as I could.

Weather willing, at lunch on many days I would sit out by the Chicago River and read. I was a bit of a science geek. While I had proficiencied out of taking any hard science in college, I had a deep interest in the subject and found some of it really fascinating. This summer I was reading "The ABCs of Relativity." It was a great book and helped me understand a bit of physics in at least a conversational way. To be honest, in my daily life here in the coding department it was not at all remotely likely that I would every enter into an actual conversation with an actual human about this particular topic, but hey, a guy needs to be prepared for all possibilities. Right? You just never know when you might need to have a working or even conversational knowledge of relativity. Perhaps in some urgent physics emergency. Hey, these kinds of things can happen in our Brave New World, right?

One day, Supervisor Candace came up to my desk. I noted that she had nothing in her hands. Hmm. No questionnaires. No red pencils. Nothing. She wasn't smiling. So that, too, was comforting. I mean with someone like her, a smile would likely equate with harm.

But she must have wanted to say something. I flashed a look of concern. What could she be doing? Thinking? Wanting to say? Hey, maybe she had a question about relativity? An urgent physics emergency? Okay, possibly not.

Candace, with her usual dead eyes, slowly stated, "The head of the Medical Services Group wants to speak with you," slowly adding, "Right now."

Oh crap! I thought I must be in some sort of huge trouble. What did I do? Did I code something incorrectly? Am I going to lose my job? It must be something like that. I had worked briefly on one of their projects, but ... oh crap. I must be in deep trouble. I sure hope I don't lose my job. I need this job.

I was ushered into a conference room. A man sat there. His name was Fred. Just Fred. The room was a conference room, the same one I remembered from the day I was interviewed there for the job, several months previous. Fred seemed really nice, almost fatherly: patient and soft-spoken, but very intelligent. You could see it in his gaze. I recognized his name now; he was the man in charge of one of our lead analytic groups.

Unbeknownst to me, this fellow had somewhere noticed the physics book I was reading, or maybe, just a that I seemed to own a book. I do not know. Whatever he noticed, he thought it unusual behavior for a coder. It made me stand out. It then revealed itself: As the mist cleared, it was obvious that he was interviewing me for a junior analyst position. An analyst position!

This Medical Services team specialized in everything and anything that had to do with health care, science, and even over-the-counter meds. And, they were a part of the Strategy Group there, a team that was headed by one of the pioneers of Conjoint Analysis... a huge new area for marketing research and a really big damn deal.

After I interviewed, I returned to the coding confines. Lots of questions from my co-workers. I underplayed it; shrugged it off. Time went by. I sweated a lot. I had like zero experience interviewing (the interview for the coding position was almost like checking for a pulse). I had no standards by which to gauge if the interview went well, or terribly, or somewhere in between.

And then the job offer came: two weeks later they asked me to join them! I was elated. I accepted of course, and was to begin my new position the following Monday morning.

My mind raced. I felt I was now in the executive class.

Now please remember my roots: I knew exactly zero people in the executive class. I would have to figure out how to dress and how to act. Maybe how to be. I had really no clue at all. Nobody. Not relatives, not friends' fathers, not father's friends... nobody that I even distantly knew was a business executive. The most affluent of my friends' fathers had businesses, all right... but they were pawn shops, jewelry stores, appliance repair businesses. There was not one "executive" anywhere in my constellation of friends or neighbors.

All I knew about "business executives" who worked in offices and had meetings was what they showed on TV (in the 1970s) or in the Sears catalog. Neither compendium was known for its accurate reflection of reality.

So armed per usual with a complete lack of any reliable information, and using Sears and TV as my best available sources of information, I reasoned that I would have to upgrade my wardrobe.

First, a watch. I'd once had a watch growing up and wearing it made me feel fancy. So yes, definitely a watch! Executives wore watches because time was money and all that. Definitely needed a haircut. And, what the heck was I thinking? I would need a briefcase! Of course, a briefcase! Black with gold trim. Those are slick. With a combination lock, for keeping all my analyses confidential. Shoes: all I had were some Earth Shoes. These counter cultural groovy shoes, like desert boots were seen as very cool, but they actually reminded me of two loaves of French bread and looked kinda stupid with dress pants or suits... which as everyone knows, is what executives wear. So, I'll definitely need some dress shoes. Black ones. And whoa, I'll need better pants! Executive pants! Pants without cuffs! Let's see what's in the Sears catalog...

My friend Steve (from the poker/pizza crowd) took me down to Maxwell Street to buy some clothes. His dad owned a bail bonds place and said all his dad's clients shopped on Maxwell Street, so, I mean, that had to be good. We got down there and... wow. Maxwell Street was almost an open-air market of free-wheeling "thrift" items (read: stolen goods). We walked through the crowd: me, Steve and one of his dad's enforcement guys. Feeling extremely out of place, I was glad the refrigerator-thick enforcement guy was with us. We were the only white guys for blocks. The worse part was that a lot of the hostile stares we were getting were of the "get-outta-here-white-boy" variety. And the clothing? While I tried my best to find things (because the prices were so crazy low), every time I tried something on, I looked like a scrawny chicken that was about to get his ass kicked all the way back to the North Side. Sort of felt that way, too. So, we admitted cultural defeat and left. Later, I found some dress pants in a clothing store near where I lived. Safe, average and more in keeping with my dumbass, uncool, white-boy vibe.

My parents (bless their hearts) on this occasion bought me a personalized executive desk set consisting of a gold-plated swivel-mounted ballpoint pen and a fountain pen (both gold colored) on a green marblish pedestal (with name engraved on a brass plaque). It was sweet, and looked like something an executive would have. Must have been in a TV show.

Before I left the coding department, I was told by one of the other coding supervisors that this was the first time anyone could remember that a coder at this large company had ever been promoted into an analytic group. That felt doubly great.

Despite the false starts and idiot-moments I got there, and life changed quite suddenly. Being accepted to the analytic team was like winning freedom from the gladiator pit. It felt simply unbelievable. Every day now, I got to turn *left* off the elevator, walk through the previously off-limits lobby, and *left* down the hall past my bosses' corner office (I almost swooned over how he was so important as to get a corner office), to my own very spacious wooden (and not-metal) desk. For many weeks, I could hardly contain my shit-eating grin, walking down those halls. This manner of existence seemed so wonderful and celebratory that I could not conceive of a better life than this, right here. I sincerely wished at that point that it would never end.

My new and benevolent boss, TV-fatherly Fred, had a George Cloony-ish head of gray hair, black glasses, a knowing gaze, a butter smooth and assuring voice and every morning we would start with a coaching session at a small table in his huge corner office. He even had a couch! I mean, who has a couch in their office?!? Big executives like My Wonderful Boss, that's who!

He was patient, kind, and always encouraging. I loved this guy. Bit by bit, his patient daily coaching transformed me from a clueless coder into an actual data analyst. I owed this man so much.

My desk was in an open alcove area nearby, where people would wander by, and then *linger*. Yes, they would actually linger. They'd nonchalantly talk about work and even non-work things. We would almost idly chat. We would casually sip coffee. At first this relaxed and comparatively elegant behavior made me extremely nervous. Like a dog that had been hit with a newspaper too often, I kept waiting to be reprimanded by the evil Candace or somebody. "Despise! Despise! Despise!" That actually would have closed the loop; it would have met my expectations and almost calmed me.

But here, I gradually noticed, *nobody* was watching your every move. *Nobody* was watching your clock. Nobody was watching *anything* at all! You were trusted to do the right thing. People were relatively stress-free, nice, friendly, happy (and, I noted, still better dressed than me). It all felt like a different world, and here I was, walking through it. Living in it. Every day.

I made friends here, as there were scads of junior analysts like me. With my newfound raise, I bought new clothes, ones that looked like the things my peers wore, from "nice" stores. I was learning; I was fitting in.

There was a strong esprit de corps at Market Facts amongst the young analytic staff. When you are young, and if you are fortunate enough to know that you are in a new and emerging profession, and you sense that you have the whole world ahead of you, this time of life is filled with boundless optimism. I strongly suspect that the tech culture in San Francisco during the early 2010s must have had the same electricity, for those young enough to get that vibe.

Back in the mid-1970s, marketing research was still in its relative infancy. It was supercharged with the adaptation of computers, and in this early stage, only beginning to grow as a field. Like the tech revolution to come later, we all knew we were doing something incredibly cool and cutting-edge that very few people could do, or even comprehend.

We worked with computers! It was 1976: computers were extremely rare, quite expensive and the size of refrigerators. And here we were: we had a huge room full of them! But we knew that computers were the future. And we knew that our careers would catapult on the backs of the dawning of this new computer age.

To set the ball clearly, in this very early time, fax machines were considered high-tech. Amazingly in those days, fax machines themselves cost as much as a car and it took six minutes to send one page. It would be nearly a decade before the first Mac would debut. And we had computers!

In this very early time, we got daily practical and hands-on learning with our big, expensive and rare computers. We got to do data processing, and what we even today call programming/coding, using very primitive machine language of the time. The best thing was that for some of us, the access to these tools was sort of an "all you can eat" buffet. Our bosses encouraged it. And some of us just plain pigged out on all this stuff.

We knew this was significant. We analysts became adept with Boolean logic and advanced statistics – the sorts of things that none of us had anticipated. We would tell our outside-work friends about what we did, and they would politely nod, and change the subject. With glazed eyes and decreasing interest in what we were blabbering on about, even our best friends only had vague understandings what the hell we did all day.

As one might imagine, for those of us who dove deep into this new field, our experience and comfort with these topics put us at least 5-10 years ahead of everyone in the workforce in respects to computer technology. The head of our group, a pioneer in many advanced types of analysis, encouraged our participation, experimentation and curiosity. It is impossible to overstate the importance of this freedom for those of us with the appetite for it: this cultural bias for encouraging us to play with these giant, futuristic tools of technology had a huge and permanent effect on my relationship with technology, my comfort with the future, and the next 40+ years of my career.

Just one example of such "technology play" might suffice: our company had a huge information base of household panel data from US consumers: people had given them all sorts of input on their demographics, interests, hobbies and psychographics dealing with things like self-perception, introversion-extroversion and even life goals. And here is the wonderful thing: as long as I only ran my data at night (when demand for the computers was low), I had official carte blanche to do statistical runs on anything and everything I wanted on this database! It was my happy place.

As someone trained in social-psych, this was data paradise... such an understatement. I spent many an evening at the office, pouring through data, looking for patterns, developing hypotheses on the larger groups of people... mega-groups or segments of the American population who had cohesive commonalities and who, almost inexplicably (at the time) also had yet other interests, hobbies and predilections in common. Even voting behavior. It was as entirely fascinating as seeing a galaxy turn in space. Awesome, scary and almost super-human in the perspective point I held as I observed it. I sensed it had some sort of extremely important potential but I was just not "there" yet.

I iteratively ran lots and lots of runs on these "mega-groups" on the mainframes, looking at the intersections of demographics, hobbies and psychography. I was seeing at this time, what a few years later I would find at Stanford Research Institute: large psychographic groups within the US populace. Fun only a geek might love, to be sure. I did not know it at the time, but this fascination with psychography would pave a path that catapulted me to several notable successes in later years.

This whole "thing" with computers, I was finding in 1976, was consistently offering me advantage, and from this point on I sort of pledged that I would go out of my way to use these machines to their best effect, since they were key to data analysis, and because of the extreme leg up it gave me in being so comfortable with them.

In 1976 I did my first ad tracking project for an ad called "How do you spell relief? R-O-L-A-I-D-S." My boss let me set up the methodology, write the questionnaire, analyze the data and write the report. It got so many client compliments that my boss also gave me full credit and let me attend the results presentation. I had so much fun writing that report that it felt criminal to actually be paid to do this! Little did I know that this type of work – communications and brand related work—was to be my chosen field of expertise for most of my career.

For all the esprit de corps and high morale we had, in the day-to-day, my co-workers were a bit of a mixed bag. A few were much friendlier and 'hangout-worthy' than others. A few are still people I consider to be friends, almost 50 years later, as I write this page. Significantly, I shared a work space with several people who had graduated with Ivy League (Cornell and Harvard) backgrounds. To be honest, I generally found these folks on the whole to be a bit too conservative and far less imaginative or fun than all the other friends I had made there. As a whole, the Ivy League crowd seemed a bit self-absorbed; too taken with their acquired objects and monied backgrounds. But it was an education in many ways, and this Ivy League connection was very soon to open a life-changing door for me.

I was glad I took typing in high school and did so many term papers in college. I was comfortable with keyboards. At this point in time, IBM Selectric typewriters were how everything got done. I discovered that these machines had a bit of what we called "bubble memory" (discrete subroutines that were islands unto themselves) and that programming a memory module, one could type in several sentences, save them and then even days later, recall them with a few keyboard commands. I used to labor away at writing proposals and realized that much of this error-prone drudgery could be semi-automated if I leveraged these IBM typewriter memory modules. So, I worked many late hours and figured out a way to make modules for our most frequently used blocks of paragraphs, then gave those memory blocks to the typing pool (a squad of roughly a dozen people who sat in a room and typed reports, letters and new business proposals). It was slow going, getting people to adopt these things. And some typists resented it, feeling this was the beginning of the (automation) end of them. And in a way, maybe it was.

In those days all of us analysts also relied on typewriters—and a lot of white-out—to craft questionnaires and write our reports. When we designed questionnaires, we were literally cutting and pasting sections of questionnaires together. A project with a lot of revisions meant that by the time the questionnaire was finalized, each page was as stiff as a piece of shirt cardboard. When done, each page had to be photocopied, questionnaires had to be collated, stapled and physically shipped to field offices all over the country. At this point, interviewers would fan out to intercept people, ask the questions, notate or write out their answers on clipboards in longhand, and ship the questionnaires back to us and our waiting army of coders. It used a huge amount of paper, and was all quite physical, cumbersome and labor-intensive.

So, back to the memory blocks technique I used on proposals. I also did the same thing for questionnaire writing and—working some late nights—developed memory modules for standard sequences of questions on our questionnaires. Press a few keys, and get half a page of questions, all perfectly typed and formatted! In a minute or so!

I remember unveiling this to my co-workers at my workstation. It went over like magic. They were dumbfounded. "Do that again." I had to demonstrate this over and over to a growing group of co-workers. This group, unlike the typing pool, was tech-forward, and so everybody wanted in on this!

I gave everyone copies of the memory modules. This, of course, saved all of us a ton of time in front end questionnaire work, and most important of all, gave us even more time for the "fun" part of the job: analysis of data. In the end, being able to devote more time to analysis boosted our value to every project. People loved this. I rarely had to ever buy another beer at happy hour again! I had at least made a ding – perhaps even a slight dent – in business.

Back in these days, everything in data statistical runs was done with computer punch cards and computer tapes holding all the actual survey responses. To run cross tabulations, one ran a deck of punch cards into the computer memory and then waited for the survey data to be run against the deck (usually at night). Each computer run and statistical analysis then, had a corresponding deck of punch cards. At this point, I had my own office. It had no windows, but a lot of space. I had a series three shelves running along the long back wall of my office behind my desk, and being a bit of a pack rat, I stored all my cross tab and other programs on it. Each program was a series of hundreds of punch cards, each card corresponding to a line of primitive programming code. I had subroutines to do all sorts of things with our aforementioned panel data, with our studies, really interesting stuff. Alas, I never gave it much thought but the trays of cards were fairly heavy. At one point nearing my last year there, I walked in one morning to find my shelf collapsed, open boxes and punch cards everywhere. Unsorted. A mess. A lot of programming work, now just piles of punch cards, randomized and lost forever.

LACK OF FIT

Working at Market Facts and living in Chicago was interesting, challenging and exciting, but I felt like I was culturally outside where I needed to be. Precisely where or what that might be, I did not know. Somewhere, not here.

I remember vividly walking one cold and icy night on a side street in the upscale Oak Street area near the Miracle Mile of Michigan Avenue, and the Lake. I passed some old stately homes – even mansions – and a few gilded apartment buildings built in the early 1900s. I admired these elegant old places that that had 20-foot ceilings, and large, arched windows. I spied the shifting light within: moving shadows of people all enjoying a much more gracious and carefree life than I.

From my vantage point on the sidewalk below, all I could see were the tops of beautiful paintings, ceiling fans, interplays of shadow and light. Looking up at them filled me with a longing. Not of any specific object or item, but a longing for freedom from worry. It reignited an ever-present wonder I had about the things beyond the horizon, about what else there was in this world. And whether I might ever get out of this hand-to-mouth beef-shit encrusted life.

I remembered those "not good enough" days of having crappy hand-me-down clothes, few treats, and watching my parents just barely scrape by; an exhaustingly long time of trying to fit into society without the supports that many people took for granted.

So, breaking from that reverie of days gone by now, here I was, just a few years later, walking down this very glamorous and high-rent street. It felt strange, a mixture of both foreign and perhaps possible in a future time. Good job or not, I was still extremely nervous setting foot in this neighborhood of doormen and tall ceilings. I wondered where I might fit in this grand scheme of things. Do I fit here? Do I fit elsewhere? Might I ever get here? Do I even *want* to get here?

For certain, this city of red meat and midwestern values had continually felt very much like an alien culture. While I understood a little of it, this way of being somehow felt wrong, off, and not-quite-genuine. It was one in which I seemed destined to struggle just as surely as had the European immigrants and war refugees of our old neighborhood.

On this cold and dark evening walk, I thought deeply about life and the concept of "fit." Was it even valid? I thought about where I was, where I was not, and more than anything, where I had come from.

In one sense, for sure, I did not feel like I fit here, right now: It was not economic though; it was about politics and social issues: I was too liberal for mainstream Chicago. Too laid back. I drove an MGB convertible, frankly sort of a ridiculously impractical car to have in the Midwest year-round—in the snow. During the Summer, when one could drive a convertible car, why, I rode my bicycle to work! Each day, I rode about 20 miles back and forth along the Chicago lakefront. Nobody (really, quantitatively, nobody in 1976-79) rode a bike to work into the city, far less 20+ miles round trip. And at work, I stored my bike on wall hooks in my office. Nobody did that sort of thing, either. I did not fit into this midwestern town.

Where my friends sported gold chains and wore dress pants and fancy shirts to impress the girls, I wore my work shirts, jeans and hiking boots. Much of the dominant 20-something culture seemed really odd to me: leg warmers, sweat bands, disco, line dancing, glitter, booze. It seemed childish, comical, strange, phony and plastic. It made me feel uncomfortable. While I could "pretend" to like it and go along with it, after a few moments it seemed like an act... I was only kidding myself. I just plain hated it. And I was as odd to them as they were to me.

The job was my happy place. I was about now getting really good at this job. Really good. I could go through a set of data tables (dot matrix printed pages 11 x 18, in decks that were five inches deep) at lightning speed. Armed with a highlighter, I would flip, flip, flip through pages of data, looking for patterns of response, and then going back and forth, tie them together into a cohesive story. Every deck, every project, was like a mystery box. And I felt so damn lucky indeed. For I was the one who got to figure it all out. I absolutely loved this profession!

I was working hard and well, making inroads within the company and getting noticed by clients. In time, I was approached by a few different client types. One was Gerber, the baby food company. They were headquartered in Fremont, Michigan a tiny town of about 4,000 people. They needed someone to come in at a senior level to run much of their marketing insights effort. I thought I loved smallish towns: I had been through upper Michigan to go camping a few times and found smaller towns so laid back, like the place in which I went to school. So, I thought this might be an interesting opportunity. Gerber was in a category I knew something about and so, long story short, I submitted my resume and got them interested in flying me there.

They had no big airport. No problem, they said they had their own airplane – a private jet—and once there, they'd put me up in a guest house. Cool! So, it was arranged that I would go to O'Hare Airport's personal aircraft facility called Butler Aviation and meet up with their aircraft there.

A POET'S LEGACY ON A RAZOR'S EDGE

I arrived at Butler; eyes wide ready for my first trip in a private jet! Out-aged by at least 20 years, everyone else in the gate area was either wealthy or a pilot with their own plane, in other words (in my narrow world) a bunch of rich guys.

I checked in with the front desk, and a fellow who looked very much like a pilot ushered me outside. There it was, in all its glory: a sleek and smallish-sized private jet (carried about 10 passengers) with – what!? The huge head of a baby was drawn on the tail. Now, I guess this might have been expected, but given that I was an absurdist at heart, this cracked me up and doubled me over. I probably irritated the pilot's pride. Baby-head airways.

His pride aside, we flew across Lake Michigan to Fremont and their little airport, whereupon I was met with a town car and brought to the Gerber Guest House. It was evening. I entered the front door of this largish house as the town car drove away.

There was nobody around. As I opened the door, there was a living room off to the right (no people), a dining room off to the left (same... no people), and an old wide, white-and-brown country-house staircase leading up to the second floor. There was a phone on a pedestal at the bottom of these wide stairs. It was one of those 'house phones' where there was no dial or buttons. As you picked up the handset, it would ring on the other end, wherever and whatever that was. Well, it rang and rang. Nothing. Still nothing. And silence. There was nobody else in the whole building.

It was mid-evening. Not only was there nobody to direct me, but there were no directions on which room I should take, or what I might do. It was very quiet. Everything was pin pad neat and clean. Tidy. Precise. So, I found myself sort of surrealistically ambivalent: There were no instructions, or signage, or any hints that would indicate what I should, could or might do.

I went on a room-by-room search, politely knocking on each door, lest it be occupied. None were. I found a room with a smallish bathroom and a bed that seemed average and suitable. I settled in for the night and locked the door. There were wires in the closets. Wires in other places too. Wires and silence and mystery; it all made me extremely uncomfortable. My sleepless evening commenced.

Was this some sort of test? Were they watching? Listening? Were they there? Cameras, microphones. Maybe it was nothing. I had probably watched too many strange movies.

My uncle was a phone company guy, so I knew some of the closet wires looked like phone wires. But that seemed odd because there was only one phone in the entire house, and it was all the way downstairs.

Morning came. I went downstairs, smelling for coffee. No such luck. No coffee, and not even any other people to ask about coffee. Silence and nobody. Shrugging, I got dressed, brushed my teeth, went downstairs at the appointed time. A car came around driven by an anonymous man and I went to the interviews. No coffee.

I honestly cannot remember the interviews. Not a one. But I so well remember this: the people who interviewed me were absolutely unremarkable. They each unto themselves seemed the smallest of small thinkers. They were beyond boring. Dullards. Middling. I suffered through all this, and had a perfunctory lunch with a few of them in their equally average cafeteria. When asked, I had no questions. I was done. And then I left, firmly clear about one thing: this was the most valuable waste of time I had ever had. I knew that I did not want that sort of a job, that sort of a company, or that sort of a town. I hated everything about it. I needed much more. I needed a much bigger life.

I got back on the Baby-head airplane, and moved on. Quite disappointed and feeling let down, I optimistically hoped for something better. Somewhere, not here.

CHAPTER III: DOWN THE RABBIT HOLE

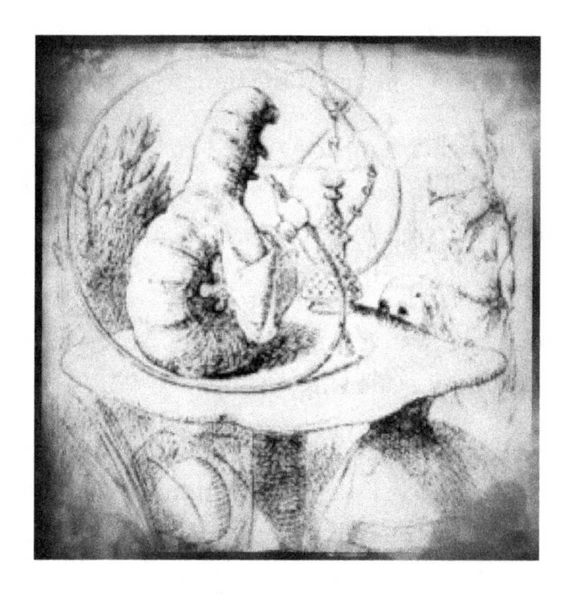

"Who are you?"

One afternoon I got a call at work from a man with an odd and suspiciously fake-sounding name: Putney Westerfield. He explained he was a corporate recruiter based in New York City, and presently was working with a holding company in Palo Alto, California, he explained, near Stanford University. This company, he continued, had lately made a few acquisitions in the consumer products category. They were looking for someone with experience like mine to add to their corporate staff so they could better manage this new acquisition.

What?!?!?

Being a cynical city person, I immediately thought it was some sort of scam. It seemed way too good to be true. I mean, who even knows anything about what we *do* or who we are? Marketing research at this point was an obscure profession. How did such a thing happen?

He asked to meet at his hotel—the Drake Hotel on Lake Michigan (the grandest hotel in Chicago at the time).

"Oh crap," I thought, "I'm being lured to my death! Or worse!" But when he specified that we meet in the prestigious Palm Court restaurant downstairs, I calmed down. A bit.

It all seemed pretty shady. And way too good to be true. And really, who the actual hell has a name like Putney Westerfield? I was not buying it. But curiosity ruled the day.

Just like a con man's mark, I reflected, this was playing to my deepest desires: with all my heart I wanted something beyond a supplier side research gig, and anything like Gerber Baby Foods. I had become enormously tired of the Midwest and its winters. And come on now, it's California. So, I said yes. Yes, I will meet him. I got my resume together, and prepared as much as I could to go meet this improbably-named guy in the Palm Court restaurant of the Drake Hotel on Lake Michigan.

I had grown up in Chicago, and in all my 20+ years here, had never once been into the Drake Hotel or even spied the inside of the Palm Court. I was both excited and intimidated, wondering with excitement and trepidation where this might lead. I screwed up my courage and prepared to meet this head-on. And on that fateful afternoon, as the cab pulled up to the Drake (just a few streets over from the ritzy neighborhood from just months ago) it felt unreal, like there must be some dreadful mistake.

I somehow gathered my legs beneath me, and walked confidently into the Palm Court: a sumptuous place overseen by a shimmering, and almost sci-fi looking crystalline palm tree. At the maître de station (first time seeing one of those, too) I saw a man standing there looking for all the world like an ambassador to the Court of St. James. All he was missing was an ambassadorial sash. This was Putney Westerfield. He was in his 50s, and had a slightly florid appearance, (perhaps had a few martinis in his time) and overall, a pleasing, ringmaster sort of way about him. He was dressed in a pin-striped suit worth more than my last month's salary, and he moved in a quite precise and measured way like a diplomat might: polished, poised, almost elegant but with a comfortable and down to earth manner. Upon seeing me, he greeted me with a wide, warm sincere good-fellow-well-met smile, and made me feel as welcome as a fond old friend, rediscovered. It was an altogether astounding moment.

As we sat down, he quite carefully gestured to the chair giving me the nicest view. He opened with a little of his background: Harvard educated, he had spent much of his career with the Central Intelligence Agency (yeah, that one) in Southeast Asia, and then had gone on to become the editor of both Time and later, Fortune magazines. Of late, he had been retained by the Chairman of this company's board to find someone who could do exactly what I knew how to do... what I did for a living. He leaned in for that last part.

I want to say I was "stunned." But no, that's not it. That's way too every-day. Deep inside, I was more or less screaming and shouting, as if God, the universe and all my dead relatives from ten thousand years had banded together to make this one thing possible. This one thing. And an impossible thing.

Was I really experiencing this? Was this some sort of hallucination? A fever dream? How could this happen? A mysterious trick? Some sort of a con? They wanted "someone who could do exactly what I knew how to do... what I did for a living." *But how in the hell did he even know anything about my skills?*

Outside in the real world, sitting there in this fancy restaurant with this fancy fellow, I hid all this. I have no real idea how I hid this, but I hid my reaction. Maybe from all those nights playing poker, was my guess. While my brain was going a billion miles an hour trying to figure this all out, I simply smiled as slowly, carefully and mildly as I could possibly manage, and asked for more information.

He obliged. It turned out that he had originally been pointed to a colleague of mine who, like Putney, had an Ivy League pedigree. My anonymous colleague had declined his offer to talk about this position, stating that moving all the way to California was not her thing. When Putney asked her if she knew anyone else who might be qualified and interested in this, she mentioned me, thinking about my vibe, my penchant for bicycles and convertibles, and figured that I was far more suited to California than anyone else on the team.

So ironically it was my cultural weirdness that helped bring this moment to reality. How strange and wonderful, all at once.

He went on a little: he said he had heard that I had gone to Columbia and had then transferred to an Illinois state school half way through. "What?" I thought. "He had heard I went to Columbia?" As if he had talked to others about me and knew something about me? I did not know what the hell to do at this point, so I just decided to nod as un-nervously as possible, and try my hardest not to look idiotic.

It was my time to talk a bit. I gulped and then—as calmly as I could muster – fed back a little about Columbia (innovative, interesting, learned a lot, blah blah blah) and then about leaving Columbia and transferring my course credits to this State school because I could not afford Columbia's high tuition, et cetera. I then prattled on a little about my state education and finished with some of the cool skills and computer experience I had mastered at this large research supplier-side firm. It seemed like this was actually working: I felt like I had impressed him.

A few panicky days later he called back, and I was invited to California. I was on my way for in-person interviews at Arcata Corporation. First class flight, all expenses paid lodging at a nearby resort. I packed my one decent suit and headed West.

The next morning, they picked me up at my hotel (a nice resort with poolside room service) in a nice town car, and brought me to a low-slung office complex out on Sand Hill Road in Palo Alto. This is the same Sand Hill Road that later became ground zero for venture capitalists. (In fact, Arcata's offices in time became the home of Kleiner Perkins.) Arcata was basically doing the same thing that VCs do today: investing in companies, manipulating them, and profiting from their mostly legal and financial maneuvers. It had just not become a 'thing' yet.

The interviewers were all highly polished professionals: suited, cultured, smart, very well spoken, and I was quite excited about their level of obvious sophistication and education. In addition, they all seemed over-the-top interested in me. It all seemed so unlikely and wonderful. I am sure my eyes were wide as saucers all day, that day.

Each interview took place in the office of the respective interviewers: very nicely appointed spaces, some with high-quality wing-back leather chairs, even the desk accessories just dripping with wealth and a refined, understated old money vibe.

The hiring manager was a cheery fellow named Winston Wood. Ruddy-faced and slightly oval, he was an incredibly warm and good-natured soul who looked like the town mayor in a kid's book, and talked in just as comforting a cadence that his mayoral features suggested. His boss, in turn, was just the opposite: cropped blonde-haired, tanned, hard looking, leather-skinned with piercing blue eyes. A former marine, he had been a helicopter pilot in Viet Nam and later flew Marine One, the helicopter at the White House. He dropped that in Southeast Asia he had done flights into places like Cambodia. That all seemed noteworthy, and a possible geopolitical link to our friend Putney, the former government intelligence officer. After a few such interviews (which went very well) that morning, they showed me "my" office.

As I stood in the threshold of this impossibly possible new office of mine, I will bear witness right here that there were no heavenly choirs or harps sounding. But there sure as hell could have been. This so-called office was as big as my living room back in Chicago. Maybe bigger. It was certainly bigger than the corner-office of my boss, fatherly Fred back in Chicago. It had a massive Danish-modern desk, a leather wing-backed guest chair, a wall of built-in book shelves behind the desk, 12-foot ceilings, floor to ceiling glass tinted overlooking actual redwood trees, and a large leather couch. An actual, deep brown, expensive-looking leather couch! You could sit five people on that couch!

Right here, right now, at this very moment of my 20-something life, if an iridescent extra-terrestrial being had floated in, tapped me on the shoulder and sang Old McDonald, I would have wordlessly waved it off like a goddamned mosquito and never given it a second thought. Yes, it was exactly that epic a moment. Did I mention the leather couch?

It all felt like some dream... an absolutely unreal fantasy. Like I had been set up. This was certainly the extreme polar opposite of Gerber Baby Foods. What the actual hell was this? Was everything like this in California? If so, I had to get the word out to my friends, California seemed awesome!

My adrenaline was going full tilt at this point, and I had to focus in order not to black out or something. I had to calm down quickly. Winston, my (I hope, I hope, I hope) new boss, suggested that we all go to lunch at a nearby restaurant. As we walked out of Arcata's offices into the parking lot, I noticed a burgundy MGB and remarked, "Oh, I have that exact car!"

Winston replied, "Really? Me too. That's mine." There went the adrenaline again, and like long lost brothers, we cruised down Sand Hill Road in his convertible MGB to some very fancy restaurant. I am pretty sure I was having some sort of out-of-body cosmic experience going on at this point.

We, and a few other potential co-workers, had a very nice, somewhat stilted but professional white-tablecloth lunch. I almost blew it when the salad came: A waiter came through the high-contrast room before the food arrived with a platter. Ceremoniously, he presented my single chilled and glittering salad fork on his silver, doily-decorated platter. "Taa-daa." (Okay nobody said that.) Here it was, looking like Prince Arthur's Holy Salad Fork. It struck me as so surreal; I busted a gut! I exploded in laughter at the absurdity.

While apparently this chilled salad fork thing was how it was done in elite society, I had absolutely never seen such an object. They all exchanged glances ... must be a mid-westerner... and happily they shrugged it off. My waking dream progressed.

As things revealed themselves during our lunch conversations, it became clear that virtually all of the 20-some people (except for the admin staff) at this corporate HQ had Ivy-League backgrounds and most had law or accounting degrees. This clear statement of that fact stood out oddly; it seemed quite significant but I could not reckon why. It felt a little strange that they should actually make a point of that during our lunch. No wonder they all seemed smart. Most probably were! "Wow," I thought to myself, "What a great opportunity, to be around all these highly educated people." And yet, there was something a little bit off about everything. I felt it was *they* who were trying to assure *me* of their quality. It felt like a sales pitch!

After lunch we returned to the office and I had the perfunctory "so what do you think so far" chat with the marine/helo pilot. I was of course naturally wanting to be over-the-top enthusiastic, but remembering my "immersive ethnography" training, I instinctively mirrored the conservative and highly contained vibe that I got from them... as I felt it was the appropriate thing to do in this environment. They all seemed so contained and measured. I was learning to mimic my hosts.

As the former marine pilot left the room to line up the next interview, his note pad sat there. I had earlier noticed that he wrote in large letters habitually. Probably a good thing when you are in a helicopter all the time, I reflected.

Now, full disclosure: I need to note that somewhere along the line as a little kid I had taught myself to read and write upside down and backwards. Why? I had learned that Da Vinci had done that to keep his notes secret. And being a weird little kid, I thought I had better do that too. Because, well, safety first and all that. You never know. At any rate, over the years I had gotten pretty good writing and reading upside down and backwards. And like bike riding, it is a skill which, once you get it, stays with you for a while. So, it was of course distressingly easy to read the merely upside-down bit that the pad had on it in such large letters. After thinking about it for a moment, even though it was spying, my curiosity overtook ethics, and I read what he had jotted down.

"Diamond in the Rough."

That's all I needed to know. I had this. Like Alice, I had fallen down this Northern California rabbit hole and if I got this job, nothing would ever be remotely the same again. In that book, the famous hookah-smoking caterpillar asks, "Who are you?" This was Putney Westerfield's role as gatekeeper to the rabbit hole. And Putney himself? The more I thought about it, the more I was convinced: he really did have more than a passing resemblance to that caterpillar.

"Who are you?"

As things would continue to reveal themselves, this would be the most important question that anyone would ask of me, and that I would ask myself a thousand times in near future.

WAKE UP, I'M LEAVING

I got the offer. Full relocation package. A great salary. And of course, I accepted the job. I then got to the surreal, exciting/depressing process of saying goodbye to everything and everyone I knew and had ever known. I got to the process of packing and actually moving halfway across the country to California. I had my farewell moments with my family, my friends, and to this neighborhood in which I had spent my entire life.

Making the decision to leave a place is such a soul-grinding and complex thing. And leaving a lifelong home is even harder and more profound. There is much sadness inherent in the act of severing a timeline. Almost like severing a limb. All of the things that you once envisioned... people, places, accomplishments that you had once held as life goals, you remember them all, at once, and in the middle of the night. You must say "goodbye" to each fondly coddled possibility in that now-abandoned timeline. You are complicit in their abandonment. You have to face that guilt. And it might be permanent. It might be forever. And "forever" is a mighty hard thing to contemplate.

My mother knew this struggle, and this moment well. When my mother left Scotland after WWII to go and marry my dad (a US soldier), her mother gave her an envelope. "Take this," she said, "and if you ever need to come home, use this money to buy yourself passage on the next boat back."

My mom similarly gave me such an envelope. It helped with the panic, but not the deeply bittersweet, confused combination that I felt of existential sadness and giddy anticipation. I hardly slept a single night in the weeks leading up to my departure.

My friends threw a party for me. Like many such parties, it was a blur; I remember little. But, much like a funeral, it was more for them than for me, I reflected. Some people were excited for me. Others resented my departure, seeing it as a rejection of them and of this place we all called home. Abandonment. I felt more than a little guilt for finally moving to California.

Yes, *finally*. Some years previous (right after the Viet Nam war ended) I had sat at a Jewish Deli on Howard Street with a bunch of the poker and pizza crowd. Big round table, the type that sat eight of us. We talked as we sometimes did, about California... And at that moment, my extremely close friend, Stuart, turned to me right there and said, "Let's do it, man! Let's go tomorrow! I'm serious. We'll get you a motorcycle tomorrow!" I believed him, as he was a little wild, had a nice bike and also a suspiciously huge amount of ready cash these days. He continued, "I am totally serious! The two of us, we'll leave this week just like in Easy Rider!" He painted a picture of us riding into the sunset. I did not know what to say. At this particular point in life, I had been drifting and was unsure of what I might do, and at this point I had little keeping me in Chicago. I was deeply tempted. But I was undecided. So, I left it to the Universe: I ordered a shake, and had the waitress bring – their choice—either chocolate or vanilla.

After she left, I told everyone there, "If it's chocolate, we go. Seriously." If it's vanilla, I stay." She brought vanilla.

Stuart left town the next week, riding alone, for California. I found out that about two months after leaving Chicago, he had made it to LA but had crashed his motorcycle into the rear-end of a truck at full speed. I heard about it third hand, and months after. It was such an abjectly empty feeling. A chance not taken; a great guy who left too soon, his life not lived to its full end.

So, here I was years later, finally going to California. Different times. Different terms. Arcata Corporation moved me, my MGB, and my crappy quasi-student-quality furniture to California in an Allied Moving Van. Paid in full. I watched the truck leave, and about two days later, I took a red-eye flight to California.

Here again, Arcata arranged the tickets: first-class cabin. I was the only person in the whole first-class cabin of the plane at this time of night. The only one. I remember it so vividly: they dimmed the lights so that I could watch the sunset across all the intermountain West as I walked from side to side of "my" cabin. I positioned myself in the middle-rear at one point, so I could take in the curvature of the fuselage and see out of all the forward windows at once. It was my 'king of the world' moment, like in Titanic. I will remember that moment all my days.

After the sun went down and there was nothing much to see, I sat for a long time in the silence of the droning engines. The sadness had been eclipsed by excitement. My nerves were on fire. I mindlessly paged through the in-flight magazine just for some distraction and to calm myself down a bit. One article in the in-flight magazine stood out. It featured a world-famous packaging and corporate identity design firm called Landor Associates, headquartered on a ferry boat that was actually floating on San Francisco Bay. It featured a photo of the president of the company smiling broadly from the gangplank. This, to me, was the very essence of California cool. The article stuck with me for years. This new land is where I was now headed; all undiscovered and all so profoundly exciting.

I had never left the Midwest, other than having gone on the one trip to Scotland with my mom when I was a teen. So here I went, into the great unknown. I had never seen a mountain. Or the ocean. Or even a real forest. I knew nothing.

I was thrilled. Terrified. I had just struck out for the complete unknown. Away from my home, friends, family. I was panicked. What have I done? Where am I going? Only time would tell.

At this moment, the exact quote (from Samuel Clemens) was:

"Twenty years from now you will be more disappointed by the things you didn't do than the ones you did do. So throw off the bowlines. Sail away from safe harbor. Catch the trade winds in your sails. Explore. Dream. Discover."

STARLESS AND BIBLE BLACK

The first thing I noticed was the sound. Though more precisely it was the utter *lack* of sound. Arcata was a very quiet place in which to work. Sounds were surprisingly muffled. I learned that quietude was something prized by the affluent elite. So too were esoteric things like Hearts of Palm, and Italian Sodas. The scent of Jasmine. And birds, especially hummingbirds. It seemed like everywhere you turned people had hummingbird feeders.

I was learning the job, the culture and the people. Things progressed well enough, and most of the staff there seemed genuinely supportive and welcoming. There were no red flags, and – best of the best – I really did get that massive office and that enveloping leather couch!

Two weeks into the job, while at lunch I had a troubling exchange with a new co-worker. He casually asked me about my time at Columbia. I answered in a sort of non-specific manner. As a follow up he asked me something odd. He asked, "Well, do you miss New York?"

I asked him to repeat it, thinking that I had heard wrong. He asked the same question again: He asked if I missed New York. Very confused, I said that it would be hard to miss, given that I have not yet been to New York and added that it would be nice to go there some time.

It was his turn to be confused. Seeing this look on his face, I reiterated that I had always wanted to go there, but had not yet had the chance. As we talked further, it became clear that he had thought I had gone to school at Columbia University, the Ivy League school. Somehow, he thought I had gone there, not to Columbia College, the communications school in Chicago.

At first, I just dismissed it away with an "oh well how weird," to just file and forget. But this gnawed at me, like a kid tugging at your sleeve. Something there just seemed... odd. Weird. Coincidental. There was a pattern inside all this that was important. A key.

Then it hit me. I replayed the tapes in my head. The Ivy League law club, all of them. Every last one of these people at the office; they made a point of it that day at lunch. All Ivy League. This fellow at lunch, thought I was Ivy League.

I thought about my consistently first-class treatment. Even after the interview, when they did not need to "sell" me anything, any longer. Too good to be true. I reflected on way they treated me like royalty. And then, there was my *ridiculously* massive office that was bigger than Fatherly Fred's office. And adding all this up, I had that sort of gut-sinking, uh-oh moment.

Oh shit: They had somehow thought I was one of them. That's why they treated me like an anointed son; they thought I was a member of this elite class. It was all a mistake. They had made a terrible mistake. And the worst of it was this: the mistake was *hiring me*.

It now all seemed so obvious: this is exactly how and why I had fallen down the rabbit hole in the first place. This was all a case of mistaken identity. I was not an Ivy League guy, and to them I was an impostor. This was the single puzzle piece that made everything fit. Everything.

I just knew it! I knew it! I was not the person they thought I was. Things *were* just too good to be true. I had entered a portal through which I was not really allowed. This seriously erroneous supposition that I was an Ivy League guy was the foundational assumption that opened the door to this job, to California, to my employment at

Arcata Corporation in California. Oh crap. They let me through the door, and it's all a mistake. *In the world of their making, I am an interloper, I am not allowed.*

"I am doomed," I thought, "It's all just a matter of time before they get rid of me."

This whole Alice-in-Wonderland dream could all be brought down to one, single root cause: good old Putney Westerfield, former CIA officer, caterpillar stand-in and Harvard graduate. He had assessed me, seen "Columbia," on my resume and assumed I had gone to that storied, very old and very respected Ivy League university. He, renowned publisher of major magazines, must have presented me with pomp and circumstance as his "discovery" of an Ivy League guy with exactly the advanced marketing research skills they needed, as a major hat trick of sorts.

With his introduction, the halo bias or confirmation bias must have then taken over. With that grand introduction from such an esteemed and credentialled fellow as Putney, nobody looked any further. Nobody... but nobody seemed to ever even glance at my actual resume or question the illusory golden aura around me! I had unwittingly played the part of an Ivy Leaguer *without even knowing it*!

Nobody questioned it! Not one single person. Even in my interviewing, nobody had asked at all about my college education. This was a classic and almost farcical case of mistaken identity, all initiated by none other than the former secret agent himself. "So much for the CIA." I snarkily thought.

This whole thing pretty much blew my mind. As we returned to the office, in a New York minute, judging by looks and other non-verbal signals around the office after lunch, it looked like my co-worker had spilled the beans and now at least two or three others were in on the secret.

So ... What now? What would they do? What *could* they do? Would they admit their mistake and undo this fairy tale? Would I be out on the streets this afternoon? If so, I was in a very dangerous place, being in an unknown job market, not knowing anyone or having any sort of support structure whatsoever.

My mind raced: They've spent thousands of dollars to get me here. They've already relocated me, my furniture, even my car. "They're in very, very deep now. Too deep to reverse course now without looking like absolute idiots," I reasoned. I hoped that sunk cost fallacy thinking just might keep them from getting rid of me.

But would this be enough to bury the issue? Would this obvious fumble just be too much to admit to the rest of the Ivy League gang? Would they lose face due to the blunder? Would I end up keeping my job? And what about my new office? And my precious leather couch!

I just hoped for the best. Realistically, what else could I do? I played stupid (my default mode), pretended all was well, and just kept on going, whistling past the grave yard.

The next day nothing happened. Then, in the next week: nothing happened. And after that, still nothing. At all. Waiting, waiting, conserving my money, I kept hoping beyond hope that things would continue and all would be well.

To my surprise and relief, things just kept on as usual. Nobody said a thing. This small cabal seemed not to tell anyone at all about my true "commoner" identity or background. Everyone continued to treat me as a respected peer. I was at this point keenly over-analyzing everything. But it all seemed absolutely "Ivy League normal." I was invited to all the right meetings, was in on the corporate secrets, and they continued mentoring me on all the lines of business. They were even spending money on sending me out on royal tours into the fiefdom businesses, so that I could meet the local management and get to know their issues. All things continued along as previously, and as originally planned.

It seemed, at least for now, that the storm had passed. I was safe. How that entire process of discovery made me feel is hard to convey.

All my childhood and for a bit of my adolescence I was seen as "less." Less smart, less athletic, less "cool" for my ill-fitting attire. And as I evolved and grew and gained confidence in who and what I was about, item by item I had overcome these irritating and unfair labels put upon me by others. I had proven myself again and again, on each and every one of these counts, to society at large.

So now here I was yet again. People had labelled me as Ivy League. It was funny that I had fooled them, just by being myself, and without even knowing I was doing so. It was sort of delicious a thing to contemplate. That it I could do this, then there was really no difference at all.

At this point in life, I finally had self-confidence. I felt that I was smart, physically able, educated and intelligent. And now, this implied "lesser" label was by this set of circumstances, proven to be a bunch of elitist bullshit.

I resented their elitist mindset. Through the last few years and months, I had developed the ability to watch, learn and adapt to just about any environment or set of rules thrown at me. It was all about learning the game, and then either playing the game, or carefully breaking not only the rules, but the game itself. So, I set out to do just that.

The longer I worked at Arcata, the more I saw how this nest of nasty, politically scheming, maneuvering vipers operated. And in this I understood the dynamics why my secret was still a secret: This corporate office was a hyper-political environment where absolutely nothing was what it seemed and where everyone was afraid of just about everyone else. Every player was constantly maneuvering for position and gain. It was a continuous war of all against all.

At Arcata it seemed as though interpersonal loyalties were fluid, conditional and everyone there was into getting dirt on other players. And what do you do with dirt? As with the CIA, if what you did is at all compromising or makes you at all vulnerable, you bury that thing so incredibly well, and so very deep that it will never be found.

So, as it turned out, each of these people who were in on my hiring... each of them to a person, was extremely insecure and afraid. And "their" mess up? Each person felt they had a lot to lose, each felt it was their fault, and each tidily swept it under the rug. Deep and forgotten. What a lesson, what a world.

A FRIEND OF THE DEVIL

This was Arcata at the time: a place run by shrewd, conservative, Harvard-educated lawyers. Ironically, despite their trim haircuts and manicured hands, these ivy league fellows were collectively a pretty dirty bunch. Exactly like the VCs that would take over this same space some 20 years later, they specialized in buying controlling shares of leverageable companies, using that to manipulate stock and make money – usually in those days, also breaking the businesses into component parts and selling off everything for as much money as they could arrange. They were corporate raiders and market manipulators, the entire lot of them; adding zero value to anything. They made money just by moving things around. It all seemed like parasitic and predatory chicanery at the same time.

I learned a lot about the importance of business and personal ethics during this period. They seemed to view business ethics merely as situational obstacles to wealth and power.

Just one example will suffice: hearing that I had a creative background (courtesy of having worked as an art studio apprentice at one time) they enlisted me into developing a brochure. When I was supplied with the copy and some possible photos, I was confused because the tone of the brochure seemed to be directly opposite Arcata's interests. Moreover, it used language that seemed extremist and dangerous, as though it might incent people to outrage or even violence.

Then it hit me: This brochure was classic "dirty tricks" type propaganda: a false-flag operation meant to paint the opposition as violent extremists. It was developed and then distributed to generate more outrage over Arcata's "unfair and un-American" opposition by the more malleable citizens of Eureka. Cynical and calculating. Dirty by anyone's estimation. But this was envisioned, underwritten and authored by these same Ivy League lawyers, in a corporate setting.

To me, this was proof positive that the people in power at Arcata were no more than clever white-collar criminals who would lie, cheat and steal to claw their way to more money. In this evil maneuvering I saw, first hand, how people who come from positions of social or economic advantage have a choice to make in many cases. They can easily wield that power just like one would an automatic weapon... to become exponentially more dangerous than those of us from more humble backgrounds.

Having seen this first-hand and having seen how power does corrupt, these days I believe that privilege is much like possessing a loaded gun: it gives you *access* to raw, and often deadly or decisive power. The real issue then becomes what one actually does with such power: the way in which one might choose to leverage power is the important, but unknown variable.

Here is the thing: just imagine for a moment that you have been gifted this power. Imagine *the immense psychological impact* of having a loaded gun at your disposal... The simple and existential fact that a person merely *holds* this... the mere fact can alter this person's thinking patterns and even their very psychology in ways that perhaps are less than 100% predictable.

This seems, to me, to help explain a lot of human history.

I often wonder about how people decide to do unethical things. Do they just suddenly say "oh, to hell with it," and change course? Or do they change gradually, in increments? Do they slide slowly into the ethical abyss?

I think that some are perhaps born or prone to doing unethical things, by modeling the people whom they admire... parents, celebrities, political figures. And some just plain inherit their lack of ethics through generically sourced sociopathy.

But regardless of how it evolves and how people come by it, the power of privilege most definitely has the ability to corrupt. I think having privilege also offers a deceptive and seductive perception of anomie/freedom: it teases people with the possibility that one can either escape or at least materially decrease the consequences of their actions, should they be found out for what they have done.

What if you had that gun, and you felt like you could do anything you wished with that gun? Like Donald Trump once said, "I could shoot someone in Times Square and I wouldn't lose voters." In the ultimate analysis, I wonder what this sort of perception does to a person?

We see the results of this perceived omnipotence from celebrities, political chieftains, sports stars and billionaires all the time. These days people label such things as narcissism. While fashionable, I do not think this goes nearly far enough into the psychological issues which surround such a thing.

Sadly, I believe that quite often the power of privilege seductively subverts justice rather than empowers it. This, to my mind, makes it all the more important that those born into privilege understand this power and equally, that they be encouraged at every turn use it to help generate positive outcomes.

The micro-society of sociopathy that occurred among the privileged men at Arcata was an interesting phenomenon. Like conditional and changing mob violence, each person and each act seemed to embolden the next, resulting in an ever-cascading intensity of evil.

But at the very same time these corporate guys were engaged in what I saw as their perfectly awful scheming and subterfuge, an army was being raised by the good guys outside the castle walls.

Karma, thankfully, had its way.

As it turned out, some brave and persistent people in the national environmental lobby had Arcata squarely in their cross-hairs.

Let me explain: The company's most profitable business was in timber products – a lot of that was based on logging redwood lumber. They owned thousands of acres of old-growth redwood forests near Eureka and Arcata, California. At this time, redwood lumber was prized not only for its beauty but because it was resistant to rot, insect infestation and was easy to work with. Prices were high. Arcata capitalized upon this, buying tracts, cutting timber and selling a lot of redwood lumber at very high prices. They generated most of their corporate profits off this business. They then leveraged this cash to buy other businesses – some o the biggest printing companies in the US at the time, a famous paper plate brand, and other businesses in this larger industry.

Here's the thing about the redwoods: single casual walk in the redwoods of far Northern California stays with you forever. These forests of the Northern California coast are unlike anything on earth. Walking amongst these colossal trees produces a sense of Lilliputian dizziness and awe offered by few physical phenomena available to the average person. Like the experience of looking into the Grand Canyon and realizing that you are seeing a hole several miles deep, standing within an old-growth redwood grove similarly produces a profound and almost religious sense of awe: it makes a person feel like a very tiny organism in a vast and magical Universe; it reminds us of how complex, beautiful, large and minute that all of creation has become. It feels both singular and infinite, all at once.

Redwood trees are often so wide that an entire crowd could hide behind a single one. The ferns covering the dark forest floor are so large they dwarf an adult. The sense of scale is so unusual and jarring that it makes one dizzy and light-headed. Then there is the sound – more precisely it is actually the complete absence of sound—of walking in such a forest. The silence is deep and unearthly, as if it were a waking dream. Every sound is muted and muffled by the immense amount of bark, moss, jetsam and acoustic baffles of all the leaves and branches.

In this revery, to then hear the sound of a distant chainsaws echo through the otherwise silent groves... this is a spirit-killing moment. It seems natural and urgent to want to stop this. Such feelings as these have motivated legions of people to save the redwoods, for hundreds of years.

The environmental organizations had been on to Arcata, harassing them in small skirmishes here and there. So, at one moment of Public Relations team at Arcata (the same ones who asked me to help develop the false flag brochure), invited a group of scientists to tour a tract of virgin redwood forest up near Arcata, California in an effort to show off their state-of-the-art forest management techniques.

This public relations trip included scientists from the US Department of Forestry, several academic institutions and respected naturalists from National Geographic Magazine. They toured the forest. They measured a few trees. And then the magical moment occurred: the scientists discovered what was, at the time, one of the tallest redwoods ever recorded. The really delicious part is this: In time, this became the kernel of a movement to declare eminent domain of this forest parcel, and to take this and many other such redwood timber tracts away from Arcata Corporation.

This was Arcata's life blood. This was an existential threat, and necessitated all-out war. Gaming this out, the act of taking their timber holdings would financially threaten the very future of Arcata Corporation, and leave all these Ivy League devils without a place to dwell.

As the environmentalist court cases proceeded, things were looking dire and best guesses were that Arcata would lose. The league of lawyers decided to take action. After their normal Friday morning meeting they decided as their first action to fire the corporate chauffeur.

They fired the chauffeur. Seriously.

At the upcoming shareholders meeting, I (the secret pretender) was actually given shareholder proxies to vote on additional financial maneuvers to shield the company's assets further from the feds. Astounded at this request made to me, the only board member that I actually liked quietly explained that the reason they had given me these proxies to vote is that I had been there less than one year and was virtually unknown. My anonymity was my strength.

He asked me, "Have you ever seen Kabuki theater?" I told him no, and he explained that all Arcata's shareholder meetings were like Kabuki: highly scripted, where feints and attestations were all so much symbolic theater: overacted for effect, highly representational and in the end, just for show and fairly meaningless. He counseled me to just act my part and not worry at all about the consequences.

In my mind's eye, I saw myself dressed and made up in Kabuki style, lifting my fake samurai sword over my head and growling, "Fire the chauffeur!" While this moment scared me a little, it was all funny as hell. And I knew in my bones that the environmentalists would win the day. I cheered secretly, from inside the evil citadel.

In the end, it all went as I had hoped. All these machinations by Arcata were not enough to foil the feds. The government took most of the best forest tracts, and Arcata itself was sold to another holding company located on the East Coast. All those evil lawyers? They of course found other places in which to roost. But nobody was happier than me to see this place burn to the ground.

To this day when faced with bad economic news, my secret Kabuki thought is, "well, time to fire the chauffeur."

With the palace burning down around them, Arcata's leaders jettisoned much of the staff, me included. By this time, I had made some solid connections in California and had a pretty decent idea of where to go next. So, like in Joe Versus the Volcano, the island that brought me to this palm-treed paradise just plain blew up. And I sailed away on my make-shift raft.

ONLY FAIL IN SIGHT OF LAND

I had been living in a small grounds-keeper's cottage on a huge estate owned by a marketing consultant on King's Mountain Road in Woodside, an exclusive, horsey and wooded place with famous residents like Steve Jobs and Neil Young. I was given reduced rent in exchange for attending to the weekly garbage can round-up, and making sure the ditches were clear of debris during rainy season. It was a great arrangement. It was an incredible setting on this posh estate along a relatively little-traveled mountain road. The woods were full of deer and mountain lions; I had a major redwood park directly outside my back door. On the advice of my millionaire landlord, I pursued and took a corporate marketing research position in downtown San Francisco at what is now McKesson. At the time, Foremost-McKesson was a marketing and distribution company with about four lines of business including dairy, bottled water, cleaning products and drug distribution. It was an interesting gig, in that I had lots of smaller brands under my insights role, and my position could affect improvement to their bottom line there. Among other things, while there I used my quantitative skills to develop a "formula" (these days known as an algorithm) to predict potential sales success in the bottled water category based on certain publicly available category metrics. My work helped prioritize markets that were particularly ripe for our product launches, and this effort further directed the growth our brands in more cost-effective manners.

I did not travel much for this job, just a trip here and there to Los Angeles to visit our bottled water marketing team. Once they had summoned me to a meeting right as I was going off to do some solo backpacking in the Eastern Sierra. I would not cancel the trip, so they booked me a flight from Mammoth Lakes airport to LAX and back, at the end of my backpacking trip. I warned them that I will have been backpacking, so will not be at all "presentable" but they swore they did not mind, so at the end of my camping I would fly to LA for the day, then fly back.

I got to the Mammoth Lakes airport to find a casual collection of three loosely arranged airplane hangars and a runway. And that's all. My company-issued, computerized ticket looked laughably out of place.

I approached the first hanger, where I saw three guys and a small airplane. They had a small sign there that read "Wings West Aviation." As I strode up with my pack, I asked, "Is *this* Wings West?"

"Hi there! Why yes, it is!" he said by way of introduction, "I fix 'em, that guy fuels 'em, and that fellow there," he pointed to another guy over by the wheels of the plane, "he flys 'em! How can we help you?"

"Well," I said holding up my red-carbon papered ticket, "I have a seat on the 10:10 flight."

"Great! You can put your pack in that open hatch near the engine," he said, gesturing. I had heard of no-frills aviation, but this was new terrain.

It was a small and unlabeled propeller plane that looked like it sat no more than 10 passengers, single file. I boarded last, and sat in the last seat in the back. As I entered through the small door at the right rear of the airplane, I noticed a small carpeted and low-overhead shelf behind my seat, where the fuselage tapered toward the tail.

We took off and cork-screwed up and up in elevation so we could cross the Eastern Sierra front. These mountains: the Golden Trout Wilderness, the Minarets, Devils Postpile and beyond are some of the most spectacular terrain in the world. Now above 12,000 feet, we started across them.

I had put on my headphones and Sony Walkman and was listening to music while enjoying such a wonderful vantage point of the mountains I so loved. We hit a little turbulence, and movement caught my eye. I thought I saw feathers wafting in the air, in the aisle to my left from behind me. Odd.

We hit a few more bumps. There it was again! More feathers! To my left! I took off my headphones and pivoted to see what in the world this might be.

"C-coo, coo, coo! C-coo, coo, coo."

It was about a dozen pigeons – homing pigeons as it turned out – being brought to LA for whatever reason one might imagine. And with every bump, they got flustered, lost a few feathers, and registered their concern.

We "c-cooed" all the way to LAX. It made for an interesting voyage and one of the most memorable of airplane rides.

I had a lot of fun at Foremost-McKesson. I made a few good friends there. And I relocated from Woodside to the city itself. I even started Grad school. But after a while, I realized that corporate life and even a graduate degree, were just other iterations of what was basically more Kabuki rodeo. For me, corporate life held much more signal than substance, and I had no patience for the pomp and bureaucracy inherent in such an existence. Further, I needed variety. My almost insatiable need for wide variety in subject matter was simply too high for me to ever be satisfied with any sort of client-side gig, even for a company like this, with lots of different brands.

Having always liked more creative pursuits, I took a job with the marketing research arm of a mid-sized design firm. The head of it was yet another one of those Ivy League guys (the bay area seemed full of them). Oh well, at least I knew about Ivy League lawyers.

We were awarded several memorable programs in which I leaned on my sociology and anthropology backgrounds to generate insights. In one project for a famous Mexican Fast-Food chain, we used classic participant observation techniques to observe, record, code and classify customer behaviors so that we could better guide the client on future store layout, menu placement, ordering, and cueing. During this process we placed interviewers at restaurants for up to eight hours per shift to do their observations. One location was in a truck stop, and that's where the trouble came in. We got a call one Saturday night. Turns out that this particular interviewer was picked up by the police after several hours of work for... suspicion of prostitution. Turns out she looked out of place for this location: a little too young and attractive for the venue. From then on, we coached our teams to cruise by the place in advance, check out the clientele and then dress accordingly in order to blend in as unobtrusively as possible. That worked out well.

Projects at this design firm was moderately interesting, but in the end, the package: people, accounts and challenges – they were just sort of lackluster.

The firm was not without some success: One accomplishment is that this group designed the iconic Michelob beer bottle. In return, this firm had been granted kegs of Michelob in the lunch room for the life of the company. This, of course, set the stage for lots of long and foggy workplace celebrations.

The standout party, I had been told, was on Pearl Harbor Day. I was looking forward to this get-together to find out what "standout" meant to these folks. On the day itself, the employees unfolded a step ladder in the employee lounge. The firm's oldest Japanese designer then came forward, layed on the floor underneath the ladder, and the others (of every rank and background) took turns dropping things into his mouth from the top of the ladder. Imaginary payback. It seemed a horrible thing. Outrageous. Cruel. It made me ill. I never went to any more of their parties after that display. This place was not for me.

There was an economic downturn, and this mid-level design firm's business suffered, as there was not that much to recommend them, after all. There was just not enough work for anyone. There were few projects, so most of us tried to generate new business, but few of us had any experience at this. And the new business people were remarkably ill-equipped for that job. While they had a few connections, that was not enough in this sort of economic climate. And when completing for new business in pitches they didn't have the requisite skills either. The head of this group would actually become sick to her stomach with panic in these sorts of heavy-lifting pitch situations. So that hurt us in a major way.

Layoffs came and, along with several others, I got the proverbial pink slip. It was inevitable and not at all surprising. I went into job search mode and due to the continued economic crunch, was finding the going pretty rough.

It was about this time that I met Ann, the woman who, after first meeting, I almost instantly knew I must marry. We met almost accidentally, at her place of work where she had been asked to sit in at reception one day during lunch hour. We met, were instantly in synch, and went out to lunch the very next day. The next day I told my best friend that this was "the one." And while I did not know it at the time, she did exactly the same. The other thing that I did not know at the time is that this heart-felt moment and our mutual decision would end up making all the difference in our time together: one day in the distant future, I would find myself in a serious situation, and Ann would step in to save my life.

CHAPTER IV: EMBARK'D

I was getting a bit desperate in the harder-than-hard job search. There were the usual crap jobs, false hopes, low offer and boring opportunities. But there was nothing interesting. Getting nowhere fast, and running low on savings and patience, I thought of the much larger and local design firm Landor Associates.

I had not called them, as my former employer's key people had always referred to them as the "Evil Empire." My first instinct was to believing these people at face value. But in this, I failed to keep my own counsel.

Landor Associates, the keen-eyed reader may recall, is a company that I also had heard of years earlier, in quite another way.

Life's odd coincidences have given me pause many times and this was one of the most impactful. The in-flight magazine I had read back in 1979 on my life-changing immigration from Chicago to California had featured a story about Landor Associates. They were headquartered on the Ferryboat Klamath in San Francisco Bay. I thought they were the essence of "California Cool" at the time. And so, despite people having told me they were the "Evil Empire," remembering that in-flight magazine story, I decided to reach out to them, anyway.

I contacted Landor Associates with no idea if they had a job I could hold or not. While these sorts of cold-call tactics rarely worked in the real world, in this golden moment I got a response! To my huge surprise, my blind reach-out resulted in a call from them and an in-person interview the very next week! I was absolutely elated just to get the callback, of course. The fact that it was with this particular design firm (on a damn boat) was an amazing plus.

I first boarded the Ferryboat Klamath the Friday before Halloween, on October 29, 1982. As I walked across that same gangplank from the inflight magazine of many years past, I saw lots of interesting-looking people, the vast majority of whom were dressed in costume. Being a design firm, many of the costumes were quite elaborate, odd, and a few even exotic. My pupils were huge by the time Em, the head of the analytic group and hiring manager for this position, escorted me down the main deck. We walked past the exhibits showing off really famous logos for Levi's, Cotton, several international airlines and Bank of America, then past the black spiral staircase at the end of that corridor, to her office near the fantail of the old boat.

Em's large office had a drop-dead gorgeous view of Treasure Island and the north bay. She was a small person with a quick manner and piercing eyes. I did not know it at the time but this person would end up saving my career through her well-hidden kindness.

I interviewed with Em and a few of the people on the insights team, and was shown all the considerably advanced testing technology they used to better gauge peoples' reaction to design. Having actually done precisely this type of relatively unusual work, using the exact same techniques and machinery for my old mid-sized firm, I quickly realized that I was quite likely the most technically qualified candidate they had seen perhaps ever, and at least in a very long time. Things seemed quite positive, so I stayed for the Halloween party that afternoon. I had a grand time and left with a great feeling about the whole thing.

A few days later they offered me the position but, with a catch: Em explained this was subject to a probationary period of three months, during which if I did not perform satisfactorily, I would be asked to leave.

I was a pretty gutsy guy at that time. I told Em this was fine, but I tossing it right back at them, responded in kind: I advised her that it would be mutual—in the interim Landor would also be on probation! I would continue to interview with other companies, and if I found a better position, I would leave with only a few days' notice.

Em visibly recoiled as I said this, with wide eyes and an incredulous lop-sided smile. Looking back on this, and knowing more about the stature of Landor Associates in that industry, I now imagine that nobody had ever told Landor that they'd be on probation! Quite to the contrary, Landor Associates had such international renown that it was quite used to interviewing people who were desperate to join the firm at any cost. Even unpaid probation was not unheard of at the time. Back-heeling over a job at Landor? It would be like waffling about getting a free apartment in SF. Who does that? Obviously, relatively clueless idiots like me, that's who. This "double-probation" condition certainly surprised Em but also made her see me differently. I was acting confident, careful and challenging—and as it turned out, Em liked that combination of qualities very much.

The work was great. Greater than great. It entailed lots of fun, and challenging projects for big and famous brands... all while working with really unusual and very smart people. But the Universe was not through with me yet.

The universe has a weird way about it: after having grinded and grinded earlier for months on my job search with no real progress, now that I had this great gig, I was contacted by a big box retailer called Computerland. They had buzz, much momentum, were in a major expansion mode and were quite "hot" at the time. They were looking for a manager of the new insights group there. I would have a budget initially for a staff of four, an area in the corporate HQ for my team, would report to the head of sales and marketing and ... it sounded very sweet! I interviewed at their impressive San Francisco HQ, where everything seemed big, important and really cutting edge. And so, after a quick round of interviews, I accepted the job! It all happened with alarming speed.

Later that day, I told Em of my plans, my deep regrets, and explained that I just could not pass such an opportunity up! She said she completely understood, and wished me well. I left Landor finishing out the week and left that gig on very good terms with her and my co-workers.

Reporting to work at Computerland's HQ the next Monday morning, I asked for my new boss at reception. The woman behind the desk looked down, then sideways and a shadow of concern crossed her face. Something was wrong.

Did they not know about the new employee? Was the CMO off on a field trip of some kind? That happens, I told myself. Crappy, but not a huge problem. All would be worked out.

She turned her back and made a call. About 10 minutes later, a clean-cut, suited and younger fellow who I had not met during my in-person interviews came out to reception and introduced himself as the Chief Financial Officer.

Okay, I thought. A different c-suite guy, but hey this is interesting.

Then thunder struck: Chief Marketing Officer (my new boss) had been terminated on Friday. I would be reporting to this fellow, the CFO now.

I was quite concerned.

I was shown my office area. It was a wide spot in the hallway. I was staring at a hodge-podge of four (not five) loosely crowded desks and a dog's breakfast of unassembled computer equipment: all tangled wires, scattered, unpowered, with peripherals in odd piles. It reminded me of post-apocalyptic junk sculpture. Everything needed to be hooked up, booted up and generally smacked hard, into this year. Definitely Strike Two.

Not to be thwarted, I jumped in and got things going. I was already on pretty good terms with computers of all sorts so knew how to get things connected and working. I assembled a workstation, hooked into their mickey mouse network, and got to the task at hand: learning about the company, reading orientation binders, et cetera.

Quite a morning so far.

My new boss (the CFO) took me to lunch. At lunch he told me about himself (he was an accounting guy who loved golf) and openly admitted he had no experience with marketing or sales or consumer insights. I, on the other hand, was a hiker/bicycler/kayaker who loved computers. I concluded that I had less than zero things in common with this joker.

Then things got significantly weirder. He (an accounting guy who would have been just terrible at sales) pretend-excitedly told me about the five-day "off-campus" communication workshop that I'd be attending with other newish executives in just a few weeks. He explained that it was in a very exclusive retreat at a remote place on the Coast down near Big Sur. He name-dropped celebrities who had taken this training and loved it. He went on to explain that they used a "full immersion" approach, so I would not be allowed to contact anyone – not even family—during this time. It was all about "human potential" and "rebuilding yourself." It was, he explained, a workshop in which I would be taught this company's communication skills fundamentals.

Ever seen one of those killer clown movies? Where they look almost but not quite joyful and as we all know, this facade is unconvincingly masking monstrously evil intent? That's the vibe that was present here and now with Mister CFO. The evil killer clown was tap-tap-tapping on my shoulder at this point. I was getting panicked.

In fact, I was in utter disbelief at this point. I sort of fumbled with what the hell I might say in response to this, and then found these words coming out of my mouth: "You know, Bob (or whatever the crap your name is) I do not really have any interest at all in 'rebuilding myself' at this point. I have pretty good skills in communicating, and have been quite successful in the business world for a decade. So, I just don't think I will be going to that seminar. Bob."

Silence from Bob. Stony face. Fakey smile.

Bob explained, "all senior leadership goes to this. It is mandated by the CEO."

I felt like I was a little kid at a dinner table and someone was telling me that "good boys eat their peas." Clearly, I was not going to eat Silent Bob's freakin' peas, no matter how much butter was artificially injected into them. And this had turned into a very bizarre and uncomfortable luncheon.

I asked a little more about the people who ran this training. He explained that "A friend of the CEO does this," and gave me the name of the seminar guy. I wrote down the name. He explained that the fellow was a life coach who had a growing following that included several famous persons. He rattled off their names.

That evening after work, I went to my local bookstore and found out who this fellow was. This fellow's name: "Werner Erhard." The founder of EST.

EST was, frankly, a sort of cult. And this guy seemed fringy and phony. In these times neither he (as revealed later, a former encyclopedia salesman) nor the training (which was later widely thought of as so much snake oil) had yet been discredited. I just thought it seemed like ridiculous, bogus nonsense. And... pretty creepy. There was literally no way that I was ever going to go down this alley. But here I was, after one day, regretting my decision to leave Landor Associates just to join this freak show of a company.

So here I was: in the position of now quitting two jobs in about three business days. What a disaster!

I talked it over with my soon-to-be-wife Ann, and by noon on Tuesday, heart in my mouth, I found a phone booth during a mid-morning break and called Em at Landor. I just ripped the band-aid off. I told her about EST, and came as close to I have ever come to actually begging... I asked her to please let me come back. Luckily, she had heard of Werner Erhard and EST, and while underplaying her shock and amusement about the whole thing, to my relief and great fortune, she immediately agreed to let me come back to Landor. I immediately quit Computerland. I just walked back in, approached Silent Bob and quit. Simple. Adamant. In Bob's face, actually. I was quite clear about the "why," and came back to Landor the very next morning.

Em gave me a second chance: she first hired me and charitably, rehired me. Second chances come rarely, if ever. This was a favor, a kindness, and another pivotal moment in my career. I was incredibly relieved to have had this second chance... and after that, I was never more loyal to any other boss or company during the rest of my career than I was to Em and Landor. Not only did she save me, but she also let me back into a position in the business world which would loom large in defining the rest of my professional career.

Em was unique. She was perhaps the closest thing to a business legend I would ever know well. Almost Yoda-like, she had a unique and charismatic presence. She was mighty, but very conservative in thought, word, deed and action. Slight in stature, Em had a laser-sharp mind, a no-nonsense grit and a pragmatic, sensible and measured manner. She was quite humble, and would always poo-poo such a statement being made about her, but the fact is that she had gravitas: she could hold a room full of Fortune 20 business leaders in rapt attention for hours. I've seen it. She had a sharp strategic mind like I have never known since. And she was a great teacher. She also was, to my everlasting benefit, an extremely kind-hearted person beneath that tough as nails, no-nonsense surface.

There were five of us in the Communications Research Center at Landor, including Em. Our offices were right in the middle of it all: at the bottom of the spiral staircase at the dramatic end of the main deck of the Ferryboat Klamath, docked at Pier 5 in San Francisco.

And it was here, on this exceptional stage and in the company of memorable characters, that I would find great adventure in the time that followed.

TWO YEARS BEFORE THE MAST

My office, like several at this end of the boat, was a fairly compact metal-walled and likely once water-tight compartment. The door through which I entered my cubby hole had perhaps been cut with an acetylene torch many years ago, the margins still just a little bit rough, suggesting the boat's serious nautical histories of the past. A long and narrow room, I'd estimate my old office at about 6 feet wide and 14 feet deep. It had a long desk platform along one side, and metal file cabinets along the other.

I sat with my back to the file cabinets. As a skier, this had its benefits. Remembering that this was a boat, floating in the bay, when storms were coming in the boat would rock and my cabinets would roll open: hitting the back of my chair abruptly, supplying me with a physical and, if I was drinking coffee, sometimes comical early warning of upcoming snowstorms that would soon hit the Sierra. In this manner, I would have a full day's advance notice (even before the weather men) to plan to head for the hills, and the incoming fresh powder.

My office window looked north across a few old and decaying pier pilings. I usually had gulls, sea lions and seals popping up now and then as company. The pier down the line (I think it was Pier 7) occasionally had a boat next to it. I enjoyed gull calls, sea lion grunts, and the sound of boats plying the bay. It was a relaxing setting, and gave me a very calm and nautical setting... just one of the views I could have at lunchtime if the sun was not out by noon. Otherwise, I'd eat at one of the open sundecks of on the fore or aft ends of the boat, each with its own bayside ambiance.

At this point, let me introduce you to Earl, our gray-haired, faded overalls-wearing handyman. He had a noteworthy walrus mustache, the epic type you might spy on an old cough syrup bottle. Earl was our patient, long-suffering, sometimes stooped, perpetually tired but highly competent fixer and mover of all things on the boat. And as anyone who knows anything about boats will attest, this sort of work is never done. Earl was almost always involved in some project or other, somewhere on the boat.

One afternoon, I was sitting at my window and heard some banging in the hold, below deck. I thought it must be Earl moving some storage boxes or other equipment about. (He forever seemed to be doing that sort of thing.) But this time I noticed something odd outside my window: the old rotten pier pilings – they were jerking back and forth in the water. Again, and again. All of them, in unison!

The banging continued. While the boat was stationary, I slowly realized that the water was more or less stationary too, and that it was not the *pilings*, but instead the *earth* that was moving! This was an earthquake!

Okay, being on a boat in an earthquake seemed relatively safe. But the problem for us was, of course, in certain places, and on most days, the boat was actually attached to the land. We had six ropes that tied the boat to the piers. These were, of course, managed so as to have "play" in them, to accommodate the twice daily ebb and flow of the tide. We also had a 30-foot gangplank through which we all entered and exited the ship. It had wheels on both the shore and boat ends, allowing it to also move with the tides.

This was the problem. I raced to the front of the boat, to see the gangplank ... it had come free from the mainland and was dangling quite wet, in the water of the bay! Our mooring ropes were secure, but the act of leaving the boat would at this point involve quite a big leap, or perhaps a bit of a swim. What boaters call a "wet exit."

Fortunately, this particular quake was not all that bad, only a 6.4 centered in the East Bay... and there had been no significant damage here in the city. The phones were working, so that was a positive step. Assured that help was on the way to rescue us on the boat, we set out to make sure that we had provisions, and that all mechanical lines (water, power, sewage) were still intact. All was good. And given that Landor was what one might call a "party-forward" organization, we had plenty of various adult beverages at hand, to keep us from panicking, or dying of dehydration. Safety first! Crisis averted.

This was Walter Landor's company. An immigrant with a sophisticated accent that often defied explanation, Walter was an amazing leader. A cheery fellow, Walter stood about 5'8" at most, and had a mop of thick white hair. He talked in a succinct and thoughtful manner. Almost clipped, but in a friendly and jolly way, like he knew what we wanted to say and then expressed that in the most efficient manner possible, many times with a slightly conspiratorial tone, as if he was telling you one of the great Secrets of the World. This accomplished, Walter would then pause with a raised eyebrow or a slight smile as if to consider what you had to say about all this. He was easily as charming as all that.

By the time I joined, Walter was our designer emeritus. With all my great experiences there, I did not get to work at all with Walter himself. He had an office on the second deck (right above Em's office), adjacent to the large main conference room at the rear of the boat. As befitting him, Walter's office had expansive windows looking north and east. Walter was around quite often: he would pop in to design critique sessions, client presentations, and of course, the many parties we hosted on the boat. Walter was great at posing deep and penetrating questions. He used declarative sentences often when talking about design. He had several beliefs on what he felt was 'good design' and most if not all of the senior people knew these rules by heart and followed them pretty faithfully. This was Walter's shop.

One of my favorite places to explore on the boat was his packaging museum. I can still see that brown sign with gold hand-painted lettering in my mind's eye... a directional sign which pointed up some metal stairs. It was in the pilot house, and sadly many of the old packages were becoming faded with the sun. Walter respected history and believed in paying homage to the past. That said, it is very satisfying to see that after all the years away, the Klamath has come home to Pier 5. Walter's ghost must surely walk those halls still.

As my career and visibility at Landor grew, I realized that I needed to up my wardrobe game from the hippy hiker to that of a more worldly guy. I observed everything in San Francisco closely, like that of an explorer to a strange land and culture. I approached this like an anthropologist. I took nothing at face value and dug into every corner of what it was to live in San Francisco in the mid-80s. I observed that in the mid-80s, 'casual Fridays' meant that gentlemen could wear sport coats, preferably blue double-breasted blazers, with khaki pants and blue-and-white striped long-sleeve shirts. Oxford cotton cloth. Ties ... why they could be any color you wanted! Man, that's casual! In the mid-80s, San Francisco was known for its sophistication and its' many-layered sartorial aspects. I wanted to fit into this creative and extremely interesting world. So, I bought quite a few three-piece suits, wing tips, shoe polish and a vast array of designer and (mostly) understated neckties. And, of course, a double-breasted blue blazer for casual Fridays!

Landor specialized in corporate and brand identities, packaging, and retail design for some of the world's biggest brands. British Airways, Allied Van Lines, Bank of America, and many European brands were recurring clients. We differentiated ourselves from all other design firms by talking about "strategic" designs that were more than just well-designed logos – they were solutions to business problems. A cause first championed by Walter and then carried on principally by Em and our small analysis team, we took deliberate care to understand the business so that when required, our work was more than just pleasing design: it seriously addressed and solved real-world business problems. The wonderful thing for my team was that our small analytic crew constituted the heavy-lifting "strategic'" part in "strategic design." In this manner, we worked across all the different design specializations, and (enormously fun for us) we had the opportunity to work on these issues all across the entire world.

Showmanship was key at Landor... appropriate for a sparkling and dramatic sort of company that was headquartered on a ferry boat. Our presentations were known for their distinctiveness, panache and elegance. We used 35mm photo slides a lot (quite unusual in the day), and all our presentations had a slide-heavy aspect to them. Rather than just single slides, we were extreme: we used side-by-side projectors, so that we conducted informative and highly conceptual wide-screen presentations with the same drama that you would see in a movie theater. This "big screen" drama further amped the essential drama of our presentation events.

This required element of showmanship put a lot of demand on the presenter. Manning your dual "clickers," it meant you had to have both concentration on your "script" as well as focused powers of memorization to know which slides to advance, which to hold steady, and at which point during the show. We believed in practice and rehearsal. I learned the importance exceedingly tight preparation. I think the phrase "practice until it is impossible to do it wrong" was created to explain our highly disciplined and theatrical approach.

Landor had a quite massive visual slide library rivaling that of any of today's online repositories, and a computer/slide imager the size of a sectional couch that basically could render just about any weird diagram one could imagine. These things were right up my alley, and I quickly became known for producing odd and engaging visual presentations. The combination of my creative visual skills and Landor's innate propensities were a perfect combination. I absolutely loved this, and was exactly where I wanted to be. In time, I comfortably took over the management of this slide/photography/imaging service group.

Landor had a process: When we were awarded programs, our first efforts were aimed at getting to know the companies. We would do a comprehensive review of all their relevant marketing research. It was like the "discovery" phase that lawyers have. Sometimes they had little research evidence, other times they would send a pallet of banker's boxes! But in each case, we would synthesize all their institutional knowledge, study this like it were course work in grad school, and in that process, we would come to know what they knew. Sometimes we'd know more. And as a fabulous side-benefit, we would get to learn enormous amounts about lots of different brands and categories. It was a wonderful education!

We would also conduct in-person management interviews. Sometimes globally. In most cases that meant that a few of us senior people on the project team would talk with their most senior people behind closed doors... for hours. We'd promise them complete confidentiality and ask them all sorts of deep and philosophical questions. It was nothing short of amazing. We'd ask them about boardroom politics, and we would play their confessors. And they'd always answer us. The information that we had access to! When our sessions were concluded, we'd disappear into town cars and limos and fly home. It was absolutely unreal, we held so many secrets.

It was a heady time. Barely 30 years old, I was working with many Fortune 100 brands in the US, and going far beyond—routinely traveling to London, Mexico City, Sao Paulo and the like. Talking with the CEOs of major companies. We'd usually travel by limos and town cars. We'd meet with the top of the top: very wealthy people, elites, board members, c-level sorts of people who would visit us, or invite us for chats, or breakfast, or dinner.

Like the rest of my squad, I learned to look people dead in the eye, tell them with gravitas that we knew their business and struggles. We were well-schooled in just about every category, courtesy of all our research reviews from previous clients. And armed with our rock-solid Landor guarantee, people were quite willing to play along, and gave us almost celebrity status.

Even writing about it now, this seems like someone else's life. Except: it was my life; it was real. Once a long-haired punk getting questioned about a murder by an associate, then mistakenly brought to California because someone thought I was somebody else, I was now a three-piece suit wearing international marketing consultant. Total socioeconomic whiplash.

What a trip.

The people I worked with were, like the entire situation, much larger than life. Much of the time I worked with the packaging design team. Jim was the lead design guy there, and had the sort of grizzled, lean and no-nonsense manner that let you know he'd seen it all. Perpetually grumpy, he seemed either fed up or out-and-out disgusted with everything and everybody.

Lord Jim's management style was quite Caligulan — he was sort of an equal-opportunity mental terrorist—he gleefully threw everyone in the room into the gladiator pit. Designers, like 10 at a time on occasion, would all be given the same assignment. After a day or so, "Crit sessions" would be held, when everyone's work would be pinned onto a board. And the public flogging would commence. Only the "best work" survived, as judged by Lord Jim—creative director and sole arbiter of his variable and volatile standards of good design.

Information-rich phrases as vague as "I just don't like it" or "it's not working for me" were generously offered by Lord Jim to the less worthy designers. I can only imagine that these poor souls lost a lot of sleep trying in vain to imagine specifically what in the world he wanted, what in the world they had done wrong, and whether they might ever get into his "good graces," whatever that might be. Sometimes the phrase "there's enough design here for two packages," was levied.

It was a brutal process, not for the thin-skinned, for sure. And because often the feedback was too vague to be helpful, these sorts of comments left the designers with little coaching or hope for the future. Each and every assignment I was involved in went this way. I saw the same designers ripped and flayed in the public square, time after time. It was a hard life for them. And for some, I privately wondered what in the world they had done, or had not done, to deserve such mean-spirited treatment.

Our core team on the packaged goods side of the business, aside from Lord Jim, included Cowboy Bill our new business pitchman, and Dean, our brilliant, eager and eternally good-natured assistant-in-arms, who researched companies, teams, opportunities and competitors. In those situations when Jim could not serve as CD we could lean on Kari, our 5-foot-tall, machine-gun talking associate CD, who in manner and disposition came across more like a hyper-caffeinated lawyer than a creative person. But she impressed CMOs in droves. And she was a ton nicer to deal with than Lord Jim could ever be even on his best days.

We – the full team listed above—pitched Coca-Cola to redo their packaging program. It was huge, and an all-hands-on-deck situation. It involved a few of our most talented and well-spoken designers, too. The pitch for this one was highly competitive; I believe at first there were about six firms in the running. Then three. Then two. Stayin' alive! The final presentation loomed large.

We all knew something was odd, awkward, somehow wrong with their packaging system but couldn't quite come to terms with it. I remember sitting in my office on the Klamath, with index cards and cans of Coke in all varieties.

Back in those days, I had the habit of relying on scads of index cards and push pins to organize and reorganize all my thinking. I did this with everything: questionnaires, research reviews, branding issues, logic and design puzzles, even when developing presentations and research programs. It was how I worked. With a corkboard wall and about a million push pins now lining my office, I had the different types of concepts or ideas notated and outlined. I used colored markers and sometimes string to sort them out. It looked like the office wall of a TV detective with photos of suspects and yarn connecting the people. I'd stare at my wall. Other people would come in, and we'd stare together.

And on this particular assignment, on one stare session it hit me: there was a major disconnect between how consumers would sort the colas (what I termed the Hierarchy of Consumer Importance) versus how Coke's color scheme implied a hierarchy. Specifically, consumers would think of diet and regular as the most important categories. Makes sense, right? But here's the thing: Coca-Cola's own packaging system, when you broke it down and stared at the colors and shapes, used a slightly different implied hierarchy. Their system had grown by topsy. Organically, bit by bit. Item by item. So, when you looked at it rationally, organizationally, this made no sense: their topsy design system inadvertently made Caffeinated and Non-caffeinated as the biggest differences. And it made Diet and Regular coke sometimes hard to distinguish between.

We had seen in the marketplace that when Campbell's Soup had developed a more consumer-friendly graphic organization and then instituted a plan-o-gram to organize their shelf-set better, their sales went up a couple of percentage points. When you are Campbell's, that is huge! We also saw that with Stouffers' Lean Cuisine. While one Stouffer's design strategy had previously been to make everything the same to achieve a "large orange wall" and increase the dwell time while people perused the shelf set to "graze" the section, we found that when they revised the photography and packaging to more cleanly differentiate and make it easier for consumers, their numbers of the best-selling SKUs quickly shot up. And the trade-off was more than worthwhile.

So, with Coke, the packaging "system" that had evolved without any systems logic was in violation of what the consumer needed. In the Hierarchy of Consumer Importance, it is vital to communicate the most important things first and prominently, in order to make the process as frictionless as possible, and to avoid purchase errors.

When we showed this design-driven issue at our final presentation, they told us this was an insight that they had not seen previously. We proved out the hierarchy with some consumer card sort data, and then made some recommendations based on that information. Our proposed design solution solved an unmentioned but recurring 'mistaken purchase' issue that had not even been in the brief. While they gave us the business for many very good reasons, this wrinkle helped by demonstrating our ability to look at things strategically, go further, and proved our commitment to them. Maybe they already knew this before we presented it, maybe they did not. But when we presented it, someone actually slapped the table when we showed them this analysis. The room seemed to pivot. It was one of those moments you get in a new business pitch where you feel like you turned the tides.

We went back to SF; six of us Landor pirates. We all smoked cigarettes (those of our big tobacco client Phillip Morris), drank hard liquor (that of another faithful client) and played cards. We took over the back of the airplane, reversed the seats (you could do that in those days) and turned that section of our United flight into our own transcontinental card room. Not at all sure of our fate in this new business pitch but glad to have done what we did, we partied hard almost coast-to-coast, all the way from Atlanta to San Francisco.

I remember the moment we got the call, about a week later aboard the Klamath. I was sitting in Cowboy Bill's office, and the CMO from Coca-Cola called. Bill's eyes went huge. It was a brief call, and Cowboy Bill held the phone out so that Dean and I could share in this fragile moment. Yes. Yes. The CMO was talking about procedural next steps. We exchanged excited glances. We had won. It was hard to stay quiet until the call ended, or contain grins so wide that our eyes hurt and our faces almost cracked. After hanging up the call, we yelled our heads off, laughing, leaping and whooping... and everyone within earshot (pretty much the entire upper deck of the Klamath) came pouring through Cowboy Bill's office doors to share in the epic news. It was jubilant, electric. We had just landed the biggest goddamn fish in the sea. Champagne appeared. Toasts were made. And the afterglow lasted for hours.

The next day, as we got to work planning out the many-faceted project with the larger team, Cowboy Bill was noticeably glum. After everyone went off to begin their individual efforts in earnest, lingered behind. I asked Bill if he was okay and he stopped for a beat. He exhaled fast, then inhaled slowly, and almost whispered, "Sundance, how the hell are we ever going to top this?" It was going to be a hard act to follow, for sure.

ROD KELLER

THAT TIME THEY PAINTED THE GRASS BLUE

At Landor most programs were broken into three phases. The first phase was to analyze the situation and develop our strategies. The second was all about doing a ton of design exploration to solve the business problem(s). The third was implementation of the chosen design alternative.

In the first phase, sometimes it was exclusively about business strategy. Other times it also included market visits to more thoroughly understand the unique pressures and conditions faced in multi-market situations. Often it included significant consumer research to get at the basic issues ahead of time. In Coca-Cola's Phase One, I developed a deep respect for how quant-oriented the company was, and how strategic it had been. I learned of entire lines of business developed to operate at a loss, and put in place only as maneuvers to keep competitors in peril. I learned a lot about corporate strategy on a global scale. And this appreciation for their thorough analytic approach made what I was about to witness ever more head-scratching.

As our work for Coca-Cola proceeded from the first stage into the next stage (design exploration and refinement) we got thrown a curve: people within the client organization were formulating a new flavor that would go head-to-head against Pepsi. This was driven by a new global leadership and notably one person who had no real understanding of the American marketplace, or Coca-Cola's heritage within the American experience. This new formulation was designed to be a lot sweeter and designed to have a similar taste profile to that of Pepsi, a brand that at the time was gaining market share from

Coke. The marketing team wanted to tweak the brief a bit to include packaging options that included "a bit of blue" in order to involve a little of Pepsi's colors into the mix.

We recommended a few different avenues of research. As usual, we wanted to make sure it was projectable and had recommended some rigorous quant testing in several markets across the globe. But because they were concerned about confidentiality, it was decided to do only two focus groups, both in SF in our facility aboard the Klamath. That happens.

Now, I have either run or attended about a thousand qualitative projects in my 45 years. But never like this one. I am used to testing creative alternatives, where one shows different designs to consumers and takes note of their reactions. In creative testing, typically very few pieces of creative work really well with consumers. As a result, I had been quite used to seeing negative reactions. But this knocked me off my feet. When we showed any of our Coca-Cola designs with blue, they lost. Each time. With most people in the room. Every iteration. And then our moderator pushed it: 'What would you do if this (partially blue) design was on the shelves? Would you care? Would you just buy it anyway? It's just a package. Does it really matter?

I was not prepared for this next reaction to the blue Coke designs. One participant, a larger guy, was shaking his head with his eyes closed. He started saying, 'No... no... no! Then he practically whined, "You just cannot DO that! It's like ... deciding that the color of grass should be blue, or something."

As he said that, every single consumer in the room agreed that this was a very bad thing for Coca-Cola to do. Blue was nixed.

The good and bad news: the good news is that Coke's executives rapidly abandoned this design issue, and let us do what we felt was appropriate for the core products. The bad news? The really, unbelievably bad news came later: the chief decision maker who was not from the US and did not fully understand Coke's iconic cultural importance seemed to double down... He had them continue down the path of making a sweeter variant... they developed the new formulation: New Coke. It was an unmitigated PR disaster. A marketing boondoggle of epic proportion. Even without a blue package, it launched to horrible reviews, consumer backlash and became to this day, Coca-Cola's biggest and most memorable strategic mis-step.

Had they only listened to their research.

GOING MOBILE

I traveled a lot.

I was constantly outside San Francisco, in places all over the US and beyond. It began as a thrill, but rapidly became a depressing, solitary, alienating, mind-numbing grind. Not only was it highly objectionable to be away from home and my best friend/partner/wife, but the process and moment-by-moment tedium of this sort of a life was a very sheer, repetitive and unhealthy drudgery. Unless we were doing a fancy-pants dinner with clients (in itself a stressful thing), the food was predictably awful dreck of airport-quality restaurants. The situations (hotel furniture, meeting room chairs, airport gates) were always uncomfortable and the company of my co-workers was quite variable: the reality was that day-to-day, everybody faced this same drudgery. People usually either wanted to party to excess (not my thing at all) or hole up in their rooms and watch some mind-numbing salve of television. But I did get my miles and perks! Made it all worthwhile, right?

At one point Landor was hired to evaluate packaging for a global whiskey brand.

When one does this sort of global assessment it makes sense to look closely at all the markets. And so, the team on this all fanned out over the globe to do shelf audits, market assessments, talk to country managers and then report back so that we could debrief each other and formulate a strategy and implementation approach that would solve as many problems as possible. My job in many of these assignments was to not only coordinate all the teams as they fanned out across the world, to organize all the resultant data, and to be a part of the field team.

On this assignment, I drew Australia! I also had another sister-assignment at the time: to meet with the marketing team of a major toothpaste brand in Sydney to do a bit of marketing research with them, and lead a strategic assessment of their situation too. So, I coordinated project schedules and did a two-fer.

I met with the toothpaste brand team on Friday morning in Sydney. It was one of those meetings in which a pre-read is sent, and only few people actually read it ahead of time. But it is a long flight from SF to Sydney. As result, I had bucked the obvious. I had not only read it twice but had organized many questions ahead of time. There were about ten of people at this toothpaste brand meeting in Sydney, and me. Talk about outnumbered!

Here I was, the marketing consultant from San Francisco that had been hired by their CMO in NYC. Oddly, it was they who were more nervous about this meeting than I was! After a while, I made it obvious that I had done my homework, liked what they were doing, had ideas about what to do to make things better for them and actions to take that would help their momentum. Everyone seemed to breathe a big sigh of relief that I was not there to rip them up one side and down the other. They all appreciated my buy-in and toward the end of the day, arranged that we all go out for dinner.

We took over a Japanese restaurant... the sort that involve open flames, knives and airborne meat. Somewhere, some wise person made it mandatory for every participant to try every type of sake they had in the place. Then we'd try to decide which was best. That was a good but involved decision: as it turns out they had an extensive variety of types on hand. I do not think we found a winner. Something about Sake-inspired amnesia. I think we closed that place and then continued to another location. I did get back to my hotel and somehow got up the next morning to go walking around Sydney, amazed at the sights.

If ever Sunday was a day of abstract impressionism, it was that particular Sunday in Sydney. I walked a ton then, too. I remember parrots in the trees, the bay that holds the opera house and seeing dingos at the zoo. It seemed a lovely if disjointed city.

And then it was Monday. Time to visit liquor stores with the local whiskey brand distributor. We visited about half a dozen liquor stores, taking pictures of the competitive environment. By noon the distributor declared, "Well, that about does it for me. Let's stop taking pictures of all this rum, and start drinkin it!" Duty called... so being a good client service person, I obliged. Those Aussies sure can hold their liquor. I poured myself onto the return flight home on Tuesday.

Life at Landor was memorable. Design, color, great brands, interesting people.

My boss Em was highly trusted and respected by Walter and the rest of the team managing the actual business. We were having some issues with our office in Japan, and needed someone to go there and manage through it all. Even though Em was a diminutive female and Japan was a famously misogynistic society, they asked her to go do this! This was, to me, a testament to her power, status and genius. When she left, I was put in charge of our insights team, our naming group, and our photo studio. I was the head of 'all other services' at Landor. This was late-1984.

Upon leaving, she gifted me her almost new Macintosh and told me, "There is no documentation. Just point and click, and whatever happens, do not put anything in the trash unless you are okay with it being gone forever."

In the first wave of Mac users, I pointed and clicked and learned by instinct how to use it. Within a year, I talked our leader into buying four more of them for our team. We daisy-chained them for file swapping and printing in what I called our 'computer commons' area. And we all turned a page. For me, the true personal computer age had begun.

Life at Landor was eternally interesting and an ongoing social experiment. When hiring people, there was an emphasis on finding the most interesting minds, almost like one might choose guests for a dinner party. Walter historically was the force behind this, but others followed suit and kept it going. The result was an incredibly creative and evolving social experiment. People like Ken Kesey, Thomas Wolfe, Marshall McLuhan and members of the Grateful Dead were known to come to our soirees. And within opinion leader circles, knowledge that any of us were with Landor just opened doors. I had access to Stanford Research Center's Values and Lifestyles Segmentation (VALS) data base on an ongoing basis largely because I was on the analytics team at Landor. Prior to coming here, I had been ignorant of Landor's importance or influence. And to think I had the gall to put them on probation! What a lucky idiot I had been.

But in the end, Landor was also a business. And these days, a growing and important business. As with many firms who grew by fits and starts, there were times in which pragmatic management meant that it was prudent to cut costs. And at Landor, there were layoffs on even-numbered years. Always before bonus time. The timing to be frank, was predictable and onerous. Sometimes layoffs were merit-based. At other times they were politically-based. Those less talented, or those who had sided in political fights with the vanquished were let go without ceremony: quickly, and without fanfare or explanation.

When I rose in the ranks to manage my own teams, at one point I was asked, with only a day's notice, to lay off half my staff of six people. Half. One was an obvious choice – a person who had been struggling and probably needed to be in a different profession. But the other two were tough hits. I had no choice, I could not let my humanity enter into it, and had to go through with it no matter how difficult. To make matters worse for me, it was first blood...I'd never had to do this before.

In later years, the ending of peoples' jobs became hideously easier. And because I learned to anticipate these mean seasons, I also learned to anticipate the culling time. One can get used to anything, no matter how dreadful. And in this manner, it all became distressingly easy after a while.

How we grow and morph to suit our ever-changing circumstances of survival! Incremental change feels slow, until the one day you wake up and notice that the reflection in the mirror has changed. It is a tough path, and every so often I run into another person who has done the "consulting" gig. And we all know; we all see one another. We share something that just cannot be put into words.

Going into this sort of business is like choosing to fish the Bering Sea on a crab boat. It can be perilous. You *will* get wet and cold. You had better not complain. And odds are, you might get spit out. In fact, you probably *will* get spit out. It might be your fault. It might be random. It might be that you were forced into a position which, when the music stopped, caught you in a very bad place. That happens a lot.

The very nature of this business is tricky and boom-bust, because both you and your company's fortunes ride on tempestuous and tumultuous waves: the shifting moods of marketing people, quite mercurial knee-jerk reactions... and luck. A lot of luck. And if you go overboard, you had better know how to swim. Because these waters often lead to a sudden and icy death. Or, a decision to leave the profession for something safer and less stressful... for example, real estate or teaching. Or hang gliding. This also happens all too often.

Along about 1987 Walter sold controlling interest in the Klamath itself to his daughters, or so I had been told. The story goes that they wanted to do an update to the interiors, and so raised the rent to Landor Associates, the company. The company, in response, moved most of its offices to 1001 Front Street at the time, and while we enjoyed the new office's light and contemporary look, we truly missed our boat.

Since the office space was not as fun a venue for summer parties, we switched to having those summer outings at parks, mostly at Golden Gate Park. We'd have "designer Olympics" with different games, the most memorable of which was where someone would hold up an oversized color card, and teams would have to guess the Pantone number. It became harder as the day progressed. We had an unofficial party at one point for our missing boat, and even had commemorative t-shirts made for the event. They were, like most things we did, wonderful.

HELICOPTERS AND DARKNESS

I was being drawn in too many directions at this point: strategy, insights, naming, the photo studio and the management of about 15 people in three different organizations, all told. At this point my focus on any one thing for very long was almost impossible... I traveled a fair amount for projects, and now had even more managerial responsibilities... I traveled to our New York office a lot of the time, trying to sort out some issues within the name generation team there. I remember, after having gone a dozen times, coming out of the Holland tunnel into Manhattan when a false feeling of familiarity washed over me. This deeply frightened me, like a flash of lightning on a dark night. It suddenly showed me something ugly that was lurking in the darkness all along: I was becoming *too* used to places other than home.

Normally an active and reasonably fit person, I was lately experiencing random health problems. It was a strange and perplexing array of things: through-the-roof while blood cell counts, asymmetrical swelling in some glands, weird patterns of aches and skin-on-fire pains. Was this some sort of stress reaction? Some weird and esoteric tropical disease I had picked up in some airport somewhere? It was impossible to tell. I went to get checked out at SF General Hospital. They did a half-day of tests. I was told in a face-to-face meeting with two stone-cold doctors, a horrible thing: they told me I had some sort of cancer. They just needed to do some tests to determine what it was.

Cancer: this seemed like the mystery mechanism, the unknown thing that I thought was coming for me, the mechanism of Early Demise I had dreaded since my teenage years. I was barely 30 years old. Was this how I was supposed to go out early? The timing was right. But cancer? I thought it'd be more sudden, perhaps less cliché an ending. Maybe an accident. Or drug addiction. But not this. I had never been anything like a hypochondriac. Just the reverse, I usually avoided anything related to doctors.

With this news, I left the hospital and walked, deeply stunned and somnambulistic, about four or five miles back toward the boat, through what in retrospect were extremely sketchy neighborhoods at the time. I remember nothing of the walk. It is a complete and total blank. My only thought is that I sometimes get this "resting killer-face" about me that if I am not smiling, I tend to look at least mildly intimidating. So, my stunned and diagnosis-driven expression on this day must have saved me from all manner of nefarious fates on that walk through San Francisco's finest Heroin alleys.

In a few days I shook it off, and came back for some additional and this time pretty invasive tests for cancer markers. I was determined that this cancer-thing was not how life would end. Not yet. And after these tests, I did the only thing I could: I escaped headfirst into work mode in order to distract myself from this odd possibility.

These days I was often accompanying The Captain of the Klamath, the original smiling gangplank fellow from the in-flight magazine article, on various adventures in marketing consulting. While he never made a big deal out of it, for a time The Captain came to rely on me as his 'guy' – a position that others (who in their vainglorious moments had decided to make a big deal of) had held. It was weird: the more vainglorious the holder of this "hand of the king" sort of position, the smaller the distressingly brief period of time before they got "disappeared." In other words, this was not a position known for its longevity or career safety. As such, I had this sense of impending doom about my unofficial status, and tried to play it very, very low. But "hand of the king?" I slid into the seat and played my hand, nonetheless.

The Captain had many moments of keen emotional intelligence with clients. For all this, he was a very effective account person. Combined with his aggressive and focused business skills, he was a very good captain. While I hated him at times for his tough demands, I also admired the guy in that he had amazing abilities when it came time to work a room. He had definite points-of-view; he gave very clear standing orders to his people. You always knew the expectations; it was up to you to deliver against them.

When in NYC, even if I had come for an overnight, the one long-standing rule was "the clients come first." Period. This meant that if your work necessitated that you stay over, you did. Full stop. You were to find whatever room was available, buy some new things to wear (if necessary) in the morning, and continue working, to get the job done. There was quite a bit of this "mission-first" and "whatever it takes" thinking going on. Most of us at Landor felt like we were expected to throw ourselves on any and all grenades without hesitation, if need be. There's something magical about total commitment, and even in knowing that we shared that... and most of us did.

Even so, at my very core this was not without angst. I deeply hated being away from home. Because I liked being home, most of my NYC trips were planned like strike-team missions: in and out, fast and hard. Get there, stay that night, work like a demon, and beat feet to the airport to board a red-eye and be home the next evening. The running inside joke among us was, "Hi we're from Landor. We understand your business inside and out. But unfortunately, in ten minutes we have to leave to catch a plane."

While I liked to do the hit-and-run trip, it often did not pan out that way. Frustratingly, things would often be a little more complicated than I had hoped or we had imagined. Sometimes meetings would run long, and ... it was clear ... you had to stay, no matter what. Or perhaps clients would ask you out for a drink. Or dinner. And since that was all very important, I spent a lot of maddening, last-minute surprise nights away, usually in the last places available... often that meant totally crappy hotels in the theater district... the sort that might have gang graffiti in the closets.

One wintery Friday afternoon in Manhattan we met with a client while, with increasing speed, our office emptied out—employees had noted a major Nor'easter storm coming in and local Landorites were all hustling to leave before the trains stopped. All afternoon the weather got progressively worse. But the meeting went on. And on. The trains stopped. By nightfall all the roads were closed. I had no choice but to accept my situation: I was stranded in Manhattan. After calling around to different hotels, we could not find a room for me. When it became obvious that there were no rooms left in all of NYC, I was contemplating which stained and Frito-encrusted couch in the employee lounge was to be my bivouac bed for the night.

Kathy, our California-based in-house travel person, had a long-standing and solid relationship with the famous hotelier Conrad Hilton. I never knew the particulars, but it was quite deep, real, and lasting. Of course, Hilton was our hotel of choice no matter where on earth we stayed. And to my shock and delight, Kathy got "Conny" Hilton to give me his own place... the Presidential/ Penthouse Suite in the Hilton Tower. When she told me, I thought I had mis-heard. And then I waved it off, and chose not believe her. But I slogged down the snowy streets to the Tower nonetheless.

I walked through the doors to the Hilton Tower thinking there must be some mistake. I was met by the head Bellman who had been expecting me. I trudged into the lobby in my now heavy, wet and slightly smelly wool suit and frozen wingtips. He graciously ignored all my various shortcomings and brought me up the elevator to the penthouse floor. With a smile, opening the double doors in a single, grand sweep he revealed an imposing and palatial sitting room with two couches, a fresh explosion of flowers on the coffee table, a chaise, several wingback chairs, and artwork in gilded frames. This was solid Versailles decadence, with just a small touch of art deco thrown in. The suite had two bedrooms (one to each side of the sitting room, also fitted with double doors), two bathrooms, and at least five telephones. Upon further disbelieving investigation, it had indirect lighting in the bathrooms, three televisions, big picture windows, all being taken in by a very bewildered guy from Landor, suddenly granted an elegant and gracious respite from the sleet and snow in the world below.

The valet left me to contemplate how I felt in the moment: tired, damp and a with a huge sense of unreality. As I calmed down, I remembered the other side of things. This very evening, I was awaiting the results of my biopsy. I was to call the hospital back in San Francisco to get the results, in about an hour from this moment.

The distraction of this penthouse pushed to the background, the juxtaposition of this amazing place at this moment in time seemed like one cruel cosmic joke that, on balance, made my impending doom all that much more likely: "Fatted calf. Give him a taste of the good life, then bring the blade down on his neck," I thought. Maybe there is a merciful creator after all, allowing me one last bit of comfort before delivering the news of impending doom.

The hour went by quite slowly. I kept staring at the phone. Driven to distraction, I ordered up some food and wine. Lots of wine was going to be handy, either way. And then it was time. I phoned my doctor's office. And there, as I waited for my dinner and wine to arrive, I got my news.

There was no cancer. No signs, no markers. While they could not pin the weird symptoms on any known thing, it was definitely not cancer. The likely cause could be some extreme mold exposure, some terrible allergy or an obscure tropical disease that I might have picked up during my travels. But all were treatable, none were terminal and I was going to be okay.

I was clear. All clear. No cancer. No doom.

And there in the Presidential Suite, above the swirling snow, all was quiet, and the world suddenly seemed to be weightless and drifting just like the dancing snowflakes in the windows.

The only conceivable thing that would have been better is if my wife had been here at that very moment. I called her immediately and gave her the great news. Then, I did the next logical thing one might do in that situation: I ordered more wine.

Morning came and I stared out the window to the street below. Clear but cold, slight wisps of wind. Snow, slush, the typical city-scape after a heavy, wet snow. I had seen my share of those moments having grown up in Chicago. And I fully appreciated how tough it was to get around in an urban environment the morning after a big snow. I thought I was stranded for sure for the whole weekend, and resigned myself to burrowing in here for a bit. Certainly, it could have been worse, I thought, looking around at the opulent surroundings. I was absolutely not at all in a hurry to leave these digs!

I was contemplating my next move which involved some lovely room service eggs benedict and perhaps some assorted baked goods. But my food dreams were rudely interrupted by the damned phone ringing on this early morning of snow and silence in the streets below. Damn!

I discovered that travel coordinator Kathy was still on the case – still working on my stranding this very early Saturday morning on the West Coast. The news: she informed me that I had a chance of going home today. La Guardia Airport was actually open, runways had been cleared and some flights were taking off. But the catch: the bridges, streets and expressways were still quite awful; most of her sources told her it was all but impossible to get there from Manhattan. Kathy then added, "I still might have a way to get you there. I'll call back soon, but pack up right away, and be ready to go quickly." I wondered what the heck she was thinking, but I (reluctantly) packed and put on a big sweater, my jeans and hiking boots, ready for anything.

She called back and said, "Get to the East River Heliport. You'll have to walk and it is about half a mile or so. You only have about 20 minutes. You're on the 10:15 helicopter, and then ticketed on the 2pm non-stop to SF out of La Guardia."

A helicopter over New York City in the snow! That sounded pretty cool! But damn, getting there was exhausting. I shlepped there as fast as I could manage. Running when I could. Carrying my bag on my head. Slip-sliding a lot. Puddles, wet snow, fording rivers of slush. But I made it.

Here, and just in the process of landing as I got to the heliport, was an extremely loud helicopter. This machine immediately struck me as both very large and very fragile at the same time. In moments, it was time to go. They never tell you about the downdraft, but it is very powerful. By reflex, I ran and ducked, and hoped my head would not be chopped off as I stepped up and into the craft. I boarded with three other, similarly wide-eyed and anxious customers. The doors slid closed, the noise increased even more, and we lifted off with an almost vertical-slight twist. I sat on the left side in the rear.

I looked north into a brilliant scene: the city frozen under glaring and oddly clean white snow, the river, all disappearing into the north across greater Manhattan and Brooklyn to La Guardia. Across the river. Out the other window... the head of the Statue of Liberty. Back again: there's the skyline. And away we go. An escape from New York in the snow. This now, combined with my new and cancer-free lease on life... I felt almost drugged and distant from myself at the same time.

DIGGING FOR GOLD

These days, it often felt like I had inadvertently walked into someone else's movie. It was unreal. And the kicker: I had not yet bitten the fatal burrito of death to hasten my impending Early Demise.

The reality was, though, that my intense marketing consultant gig came with a price. A price that I was increasingly aware of... Running around the country and the world on these projects was at times exhilarating but constantly physically and psychically exhausting.

I felt very much the absentee everything: husband, father, manager, friend. I was never around. I was failing at all of the important things. I sometimes felt like I was not occupying my body, only watching it from afar. Some sort of dissociation between the life I was now living, and who I really wanted to be at my core.

Preparing for one such trip to NYC, I got the heads up that The Captain wanted me to accompany him to a breakfast meeting with a fellow from a major global management consulting firm. This fellow 'had connections' with some decision-makers at General Motors. He had told The Captain that there was a need to talk. That's pretty much all we knew.

In preparation for the meeting, my mission was to find out what I could about this management consulting firm and its relationship with GM... and anything else that might shine a light on what GM was up to.

This was one of the things that I became pretty good at. I used to do library research long before the days of the public internet. It was worthwhile, and I was pretty decent at it. I had at first honed those skills when in college, combing through books, periodicals and such. Then later, I used to use these skills mostly for recreational purposes. I found, for example, significant archeological sites across the Southwest and Mexico that still today, are quite obscure.

I read a lot. I was familiar with all the local business libraries and their odd assortment of book-based data, and lucky for me, had learned while at Arcata to use the Lexus/Nexus network (precursor to the internet) to do whatever fact-finding I could, usually through the connections I had developed at Stanford Research Institute (SRI).

In this particular case, I got plenty of information. I found out that GM was working with people in Europe on different automotive manufacturing technologies – 'lost foam' engines, different chassis, tires, robotic assembly processes... for some possible new initiative, and that this management consulting firm might have been involved to some still obscure degree.

During our breakfast in NYC, this management consultant contact confirmed that such a development program was in fact happening, that it was being led by a fellow who had pioneered several other outside-the-box projects at GM (including the mid-engine, partially plastic molded Pontiac Fiero). Finally, he admitted that the focus here was to build a new car "from the ground up," perhaps even a whole line of cars. As the discussion evolved, it became clear that the current debate internally within GM was whether it would be folded into one of the big brands (Pontiac or Chevrolet) or might be something else... perhaps a new car brand entirely. The conceptual "mission" of this new group at GM was to change the way that people thought of US-built cars and make them as reliable and dependable as the Japanese.

A new brand of cars? This had not happened in many years, if ever, at GM. Usually automotive lines were added through acquisition. Strategically, this move by GM seemed seismically important at this point in time. For at this time, GM's reputation for quality was seen as a terrible failure. Domestic auto sales were falling; they (and Ford and Chrysler) were being hammered and embarrassed by the likes of Honda and Toyota on build quality, reliability and durability. Some auto experts went so far as to publicly fear that the future of the American manufacturing process was in serious question; that it's very future was at stake. For all of these very good reasons, all indications pointed to a massive and important program at GM. Perhaps bigger than anything GM had had done before. Possibly bigger than Landor had done before. Sensing the seriousness of the situation, this set of calculations put us into overdrive, and we immediately began putting a team together to meet this challenge.

We secured an initial proof-of-qualifications meeting with the decision-makers and marketing teams at General Motors in Detroit. For a month solid, we worked on this presentation as though it were the biggest opportunity in the Universe. Many of us were putting in 80-hour work weeks. And then we made our way to Detroit. We included so many of our senior Landor team on that trip that for business safety reasons, we flew in two separate planes. The meeting took place in their Board Room at the largest single table I had ever seen. More than 30 people from GM attended, with more than half a dozen of us from Landor.

Our team consisted of the head of our Retail Design group, his creative director, several account people, an automotive retail specialist, The Captain, and myself. We presented our credentials, experience with automotive (several European brands including our current client Mercedes Benz), our research and analytics capabilities an our three-phase process.

The Q&A session (which has always been my favorite part of any presentation) centered on the 'research review' that my team would begin with, and how further research might be done to direct the marketing effort. They were specifically interested in the way in which we would go about defining the target and the way we envisioned the marketing of a brand-new brand.

While I had a deep history with psychographic issues, especially at my time working in the supplier-side in Chicago, ever since coming to California and working at Arcata (near Stanford) I had been doing a lot of deep psychographic work with SRI's Values and Lifestyles Segmentation (VALS) program in my spare time. Through that intellectually invigorating effort, I had developed a deep familiarity with psychographic segmentation, and without thinking much about it, a casual and deep way of talking about it. I was so at home with it, it felt like talking about a family member. So, when the question of target marketing came up, I naturally and casually talked through this: all my involvement with SRI and how this type of thinking might be applied to this particular situation

Then the most wonderful thing occurred: I saw on their faces that this was new, exciting and cutting-edge stuff to all of them. I just out-and-out just told them that the thing they needed to do was to target 'early adopters.' By that I meant people who were finding the new things in the world, setting the trends. "We'll have to do research in order to find these people,' then understand them and motivate them. But we can do it. I talked about the people who were most likely to accept new brands and the process for identifying, addressing and motivating them. "We'll start in California and ripple out from there to the rest of the country."

I had hit a nerve. Or perhaps a theme they had been wrestling with. Or they thought I was so sure of what I was saying that I must know something they do not know. Frankly, I will never ever know what event or sequence tilted the table, but the more I talked, the more intently they listened. I sensed this and leaned in: I just kept going for a good long bit.

I stopped when I got a look from The Captain. He always had a good grasp on the subtle cues of clients' mannerisms. That was the absolute right thing to do, to stop. And as I stopped, they piled in, and then it became a true and invested conversation. An interchange. Our meeting became much more than a meeting; it was an excited, animated and very positive, collaborative discussion, with many of us building on thoughts, and lots of questions about what we might do. And when.

Right then, I had that gut feeling you get in some new business presentations. Hard to pin down, impossible to explain. But you just know it to be true. Innate, intuitive, immediate: We Just Won!!!

Like with many things, a lot goes into winning a project. We had some of the most brilliant people I have ever had the chance to work with right there in that room, and in my estimation the very best and most talented design team in the world. We showed them our tons of recent category experience useful not only in design but also in the incredibly complicated implementation of a new brand. Frankly, they would have been nuts if they did not hire us. They were in love with us by the time the Q&A session began. But then... that discussion! Oh, brother. It took us over the goal line.

The internal working name of their team was Team Saturn, so named for the rocket, not the planet. It was named by the core engineering team that had started this experiment: because of the audacious and outlandish goal they had, which they likened to building a rocket that would take them to the moon.

And so, we all were joining them on the launch pad: Here, we joined the mission. Here and now, Landor and Team Saturn joined up and marched with smiles and a determined forcefulness, right into the unknown, confident that this incredibly outlandish experiment would actually work out.

TREBUCHETS INTO SPACE

Let's just start over for a minute here: just imagine that someone comes up to you and sketches a plot to develop a brand-new brand for a car company. Imagine how skeptical you might be, no matter who was doing the telling. It seemed almost ridiculous that such a thing could happen! A brand-new company? That made lots of cars? Underwritten (apologies to those in Detroit) by a company that made lumbering, over-engineered and on the whole pretty crappy cars? And you are being asked to strap yourself to this rocket? Sounds damned dangerous, yes?

Yet, here we were, a team dedicated to getting this done. With absolutely no guarantee whatsoever that it would even get off the ground. Let along take us to the moon and back, as it were. Would it explode? Would it kill us all?

When all of this was looked at realistically, we were trying to do something mightily improbable. It was antithetical to everything that General Motors had done before. It was a clean slate approach, with the fundamental assumption that there were better ways of making a car. This was decoded by many people at all levels at General Motors – junior and senior – as "everything you are doing is wrong." It was an existential slap in the face to broad swaths of people all across General Motors: workers, managers, marketers, and engineers.

A long shot.

I mean, how could this work? It was General Motors. And with GM, a company which in its sheer size and blinding complexity had fits of back-and-forth, jumps and starts, political battles which could abruptly halt any program, especially one of this controversial character. A goddamn moonshot at best. We quashed our internal defeatism and skepticism. Some of us suspected that we were put on this undertaking like some soldiers are assigned to suicide missions. The possibility of success was slim.

All in all, being on the Saturn project – for everyone concerned—felt like being catapulted on a giant trebuchet into space.

The team at Saturn we worked with were quite memorable and not what I would have imagined as people who would hold executive positions at General Motors. Leading the team was Bill Hoglund, the fellow who basically had built Pontiac. His latest bold experiment was to get the Pontiac Fiero built. It, like Saturn, was a slap in the face to everything GM had done. It was the only 2-seater other than the sacrosanct Corvette. It had a T-bar quasi-convertible set up like the much-loved Porsche Targa. It used a few plastic body parts (heresy in those days) and last but not least, it was a mid-engine car! Nobody but exotic cars builders messed with that. But Hoglund was not afraid to experiment. Others on the team ranged from pleasant and eccentric Carol S, to a fellow named TJ who looked like guitarist Mason Williams if he had a tombstone beard and joined ZZ Top. TJ was a tough and clear-headed guy. Might have been Texan; he wore cowboy boots and hats almost all the time. These people were all eccentric and non-conformist to their very core. They were proud to be bucking the "establishment" at General Motors.

There were many people at GM who were waiting to see Saturn go away. I had solid feelings that several were actively plotting for it to explode on the launch pad from the get-go. I could never prove that, but it sure seemed likely given the attitudes around GM, the widespread lack of cooperation that we and the Saturn team had experienced with service groups inside General Motors, and the generally high internal headwinds that we constantly had to buck to get things approved.

But our combined team was bold and brave. And for the absolute only time in my 45-year career we actually got close to carte blanche on budget, methodology and thoroughness. Project after project, each of our budgets for this/that /the other aspect of our spiraling, ornate and incredibly long research process were getting approved. Item by item by item. Everything. When we totaled it up several weeks into the relationship, we were in disbelief. We were giddy.

Don't get me wrong, we were not wasting money, and we were being careful with resource allocation. But this "yes, let's do this" environment... well, it just was not the norm!

It was a moonshot of the highest order. We had ambitious information goals and our research plans were written to address and meet them. Our tasks were to:

1/understand the car buying process in all segments in the US

2/map the positionings of all brands

3/key in on the vulnerabilities of all competitors

4/identify the white space pockets of opportunity for positioning this brand

But that was not all. Once all that had been digested and acted upon we were to go even further: to then iteratively test the optimal ways in which to express the most powerful positioning for this particular product and brand in the marketplace.

Finally, of course, we had to come up with a new name and logo for this company, division or whatever the heck it was (nobody really specified). And test all of that, too.

Yes, it was a lot; frankly it was an absolutely staggering mission. But both we and the client team were all-in. We'd never worked like this before. And even today, I've never worked like that since.

Our only constraint: we had nine months in which to make this happen. Nine months! For those who have not done such a thing as this, nine months was an absolutely impossible schedule. Doubly so when working through all the layers of approval needed within the largest car company in the world.

This was going to be a full-time gig for me and for just about anyone who worked on this in my team. I had to hire people expressly for this or repurpose good people and hire new replacements to take their spots. The pitch was simple: It was a chance to make history. I got a lot of great applicants and had my pick. The new team assembled, our first step was qualitative work – over 80 focus groups all over the United States that covered issues such as perceptions of car brands, the best and worst parts of the buying process, things most valued in a car, and the many ways that cars fit into peoples' lives. We used several different firms to pull this off, one lead moderator and about three alternates.

We did these focus groups in California, Chicago, New Jersey and in the Southeast. The groups were successful and after working through all the data and the resulting body of knowledge, we used large-scale quantitative research to map the marketplace. Once we had that figured out and could eliminate all the subcategories that we had no business trying to occupy (a mean feat in and of itself) we did more qualitative work to develop some different angles of positioning. We started with about four and then had a few which really needed several variations. We developed image boards for the different positionings, rapidly eliminated a few and refined the leaders further in more iterative qualitative. At this time the product design team at Project Saturn had refined its products so that we could begin positionings of the brand with this necessary product context fully fleshed out. Because this was in the days before, well, anything 3D, we had to rely on a lot of artist renderings. It was as detailed as we could make it, given the limited visual tech of the time.

At about the five-month mark, we knew many things about the positioning of the brand. It would be innovative, independent, approachable, un-car guy, everyman... the car brand for the rest of us. The car brand for people who want things simple, direct, relaxed and unpretentious. For people who, when buying a car, were wanting a new member of the family. Something they could trust and depend on.

Seeing major market challenge and opportunity, we took our assignment much further than the objectives or the brief called for. As background, during this time many people had the distinct feeling that all American cars were terrible. Many people (especially import buyers) felt that domestic cars would fall apart quickly and then dealerships would "play the game" and overcharge for repairs that "were their fault in the first place." The reputational situation was dire. While GM knew this and had launched Saturn in order to counter this terrible reputation and prove to America that the US could make a quality automobile, the fact was that many at GM still did not want to hear or be reminded of the terrible image of American car manufacturing.

Nevertheless, all of the research we did pointed at the same thing: in order to succeed, Saturn would have to keep GM at arm's length, and a long arm's length at that. This was something that was critically important, but something GM really did not want to hear. We at Landor realized that any GM connection to Saturn bordered on toxicity at the time. Inside Landor, the rallying cry was to reimagine Saturn as being the "Anti-Christ" to everything that was GM. This was highly controversial, highly confidential, but widely embraced within our ranks.

The head of our Retail Design Group was a fellow I'll call Sage. He'll wince at the name, he's a fellow with disarming humility. But he was a sage, so I will call him that. While we all had fun with our research in figuring out how to differentiate Saturn, from where I sat and how I look back at it now, this fellow Sage is the number one guy who made this all work.

Tall, friendly, smart and extremely charismatic, he was a guy that everybody just wanted to hang with. In his late 40s, Sage loved MTV, sometimes wore a red bandana around his prematurely white and bushy head of hair when he ran, and had an eternally young and active outlook on life. It was his observation that Saturn needed to be housed in *completely independent dealerships*, to further separate Saturn at the customer point-of-contact from the rest of General Motors.

This became known as the Saturn retail dealership model. In my view, his contribution was perhaps the most crucial and significant part of our positioning plan. At our great peril, we took a collective deep breath and told General Motors the bad news: in order to succeed, they had to change their dealership model, totally and completely.

Sage did the heavy lifting on this one. And the looks on our clients' faces when we gave them this strong recommendation was grave and for us, panic-inducing. The financial implications of this reco were severe: such dealerships would have to be independent, free-standing businesses, with no obvious branded affiliation to GM. There could be no GM badging on any sheet metal. The plants, employees et cetera could not be GM. The sales tactics had to totally change to a passive, customer-sets-the-pace tempo and temperament. In our first meetings with our core GM team, this received a strongly negative reaction. To be honest, after we left, I felt nauseous: I felt like they might fire us over such a costly and almost impossible idea. GM management seemed widely and vigorously opposed to this due to the complications both with dealerships, labor unions and because of the significantly higher cost implications for both GM and its dealers.

It took about five meetings to work through, massage the message and politically pre-sell this concept, so that when it was finally presented to the GM board of directors, everyone would be able to leave the room with their lives intact. The fact that we had the vision to conceive this, the guts to propose this, and the dogged perseverance to stick to this, and finally get GM to embrace this revolutionary concept was, in my opinion, the most important aspects to our positioning concept, and the key elements that kept this from being "just another bit of smoke and mirrors." This retail strategy embodied the heavy lifting necessary to make this crazy concept work. All credit here goes to the head of our Retail Design Group, the fellow I am calling Sage.

The last piece central to our vision for Saturn was the controversial no-pressure sales approach. When first presented to them it, like the stand-alone dealer concept, also fell from the sky with a major thud. Even though we had shown that it would be central to the entire brand, there was huge resistance from the sales organization. They, after all, had spent their entire careers doing things the traditional way. And who were we to change their methods?

GM again balked at the costs, effectiveness and logistical issues with all of this. But we persevered and said that the critical key to success was to have this no pressure no-haggle environment as part and parcel of the whole. Without all of this working as one unified system, the brand positioning would widely be mocked as a sham, and Saturn would fail.

Not only did this of course continue to enrage a few of the lifers who thought we were telling them that "you are doing it wrong," but this was also, for the people watching budgets, promising the be an incredibly expensive proposition for not only GM but its entire dealer body.

Imagine the cynics version of the pitch: "so we're going to triple the hard costs (real estate, mechanicals necessary for service and parts and the like) and here's the rub: no-pressure, no haggling sales. That's right, just forget what you have been doing your entire career. Now, you just let customers come and go and only approach them if they want more information. Then, no pricing tactics, no 'sales prices.' No mind games. No 'lost your trade in keys,' no 'my manager will kill me but here's a better pricing option.' None of that."

Just imagine... you have a car sales business you have run for, say, 30 years and GM pitches you this sort of new idea, without any guarantee it would work. It was a hard sell for us at Landor, just as it would be a hard sell for GM's dealer relations teams.

We again persevered. The issue took months to resolve. But ultimately, we won the day. Writing this, I realize that as far as I know, nobody who was on the program has written this before. But this is how it went down. Did it go far enough? Probably. Did they take every recommendation that we made? No. But this total positioning package acted to meaningfully differentiate Saturn from every other brand in the entire category. And this aspect was squarely the result of our Retail Design Leader, Sage. This likely was the biggest and most crucial decision in the positioning of Saturn.

Now it came time for branding: We developed a wide variety of potential names for them; typically, offshoots of words and concepts from science and astronomy. But interestingly, none worked as well as Saturn. And then – significantly – there was the employee morale side of things. Many people within the Saturn Team had been working in a dedicated mission under the Saturn banner for years. They had lapel pins. They rallied under this "flag" way before there was a product. Way before they even had job titles, in some cases. This was their identity. So, the name stayed.

As for logos, we initially designed as many as 30 or 40 iterations. Rockets did not excite the imagination of consumers as the space shapes or stars, or planetary images. The planet Saturn itself had an inescapable allure: there was something mysterious, aspirational and motivating here. Almost like Mars in our populist Earthly myths, but with the iconic and evocative rings.

With the client's input and guidance, we eliminated all but three planetary designs and then quantitatively tested them all. Several alternatives tended to have more literal, conservative renderings of the planet. The winning alternative (the one that became their logo) had a more abstract design. At first, the client was concerned that it was too abstract, not traditional enough. We lobbied for the more abstract approach since it seemed to be seen as more futuristic, upscale and technologically advanced. We also considered iterations of vehicle badging that had GM parent associations. In the end the "Abstract Red" Saturn design won because of its more forward-leaning imagery. As has been observed on the internet, one of the rings had a swoosh which, the designer pointed out, felt like that of a rocket that accelerated just out of frame. Finally, we used quantitative research to convince GM to disassociate it from the parent, showing that such a disassociation would aid the brand's success in market.

We had told the client many times that this brand would only work if GM was not seen as its overlord. We told them plainly and carefully that if people saw GM as the parent, it would wither on the vine before it had a chance to shine. Personally, in one of my most nervous moments in this program I argued this exact point of view in person to Roger Smith, Chairman at GM, in our big presentation theater at 1001 Front Street in San Francisco.

I succeeded. Using reams of research as evidence, I conclusively showed Mr. Smith that the GM name had to be invisible. It had to stay away. That meant no GM stamps, no 'badge engineering' (as the similarity was between Chevy and GMC, for example), and that even literature in the car, on the dealer show rooms, in the hands of owners – all needed to eliminate or minimize GM branding.

About Mr. Smith from my viewpoint: This presentation was my last on the program as it transitioned to launch and implementation. To my knowledge, it was the only time we had any involvement with Mr. Smith. While Roger Smith is often credited as the father of Saturn, I believe this is just a classic example of eager PR people practicing revisionist history and over-painting the truth. I suspect that he may have been in the room for a few discussions with his management team, and certainly gave approval to everything that was done, But I believe based on his relative invisibility at key moments, that his role was greater than arm's length. In fact, when we first started, Smith's name was never evident in any correspondence or made manifest in any discussions. Bill Hoglund's was. Hoglund seemed to me to be the force in the beginning of our involvement, plain and simple. And at a certain time, there was a definite transition from Bill Hoglund to John Middlebrook, especially as we got into the dealership model discussion stage. Mr. Middlebrook kept up an active role as we proceeded through the program. But Smith's name – it was seldom seen and his voice was heard only once.

We at Landor liked Hal Riney & Associates' ads. Located near our San Francisco offices, we felt that Hal Riney & Associates was the right choice for the agency to handle the car account. And we made that plain to the Saturn team. We admired a lot of their work. In about 1984 they had done some particularly breakthrough work for Bartles & James wine coolers and we felt that the "common man" sort of tone of these ads was exactly right for Saturn. The Saturn team agreed with our reasoning. The Captain made the call to Hal. I stood next to The Captain's desk as he called Hal and asked him if he would be interested in the project. That's how it went down.

For the handoff, I developed a deep brand book (it was about an inch thick with all the appendices) as a briefing and source document for anyone who would work on the brand, anywhere in the world. I wish I still had a copy of that book.

The actual positioning statement was brief, only a page and a half long. I believed that if you couldn't explain a brand's point of difference in a few sentences to your best friend, it was pretty worthless. So that's the approach I used.

The positioning statement, as best as I can recall, was this:

Saturn is the car that everyone wanted to make, but couldn't. Until now. It is the car that is made with care. By people who care about you, about the environment and about the long-term. It is the car, and the car company, that you can depend on. It is the car for the rest of us. Using the newest and best technologies, fresh thinking and no-haggle pricing, Saturn is changing the way that cars are made, sold and serviced. Right here in America.

The background in the appendix of the briefing book included summaries of all the many stages of marketing research that had been done, qualitatively and quantitatively, since our program began.

After this official "hand-off" on the creative work occurred, we went into an incredibly detailed implementation phase for how the brand would be handled in the retail realm: not only the obvious things like site signage but also just about every way in which the brand might be experienced by the customer, from textures to color schemes to directional signage and display areas. We looked at the building and interior experience of the building as an integral part of the brand. I believe that we were one of the first companies to think about brand experience in such a holistic manner. We had just completed a program like this for Mercedes Benz globally, and through the things we had learned, now were unparalleled at our abilities to handle such a complex program for GM.

In scope and attention, this "last mile" and pivotally important stage of the project dwarfed, both everything that had gone before. Our design team also included the public and employee areas of the Springhill plant and all factory-centric customer contact points as a part of our implementation phase. The goal: to provide a complete, continuous, and holistic "Saturn experience" to customers, no matter how they chose to interact with the brand in the marketplace.

We still, of course, had no idea what would become of this project. We just hoped it would launch, we hoped that the no-pressure dealership concept we had proposed would actually work, we hoped that General Motors would leave it independent. This cascading chain of hopes was threadbare thin upon rational examination. And any failing at any stage would have brought it all down and relegated this brand to marketing catastrophe and/or marketing obscurity.

It was exciting when things took off. But like shooting a rocket into the sky to find a distant planet, we all knew that rockets occasionally blow up. Some never reach their destination. So, all we could do was to breathe slowly, and wait.

In our very early focus groups, we had asked people to tell us about their best experiences in car buying. We were, at the time, trying to find the "gold" in how to develop a better sales approach. But in this line of questioning, we found something more. One woman described the first car she ever bought: a birthday present to herself, a reward to herself for hard work and dedication to a goal. In the focus group she shared with excitement how the dealership had actually listened to her, and how they delivered the car to her on her birthday, with a birthday cake! In time, when Hal Riney & Associates was brought in, this became one of their very first ads for Saturn.

When Saturn launched there was fanfare. But the results? That took time. But fully five years later even the most prudent of us could tell: this had succeeded way beyond most yardsticks. Saturn won numerous awards for reliability and popularity. It had a great sales record. While it is true that Saturn cannibalized sales from other GM lines, any indication of surprise by financial people at General Motors would have been disingenuous. They knew from the get-go that this was a probability. It was a short-term hit, taken for long term benefit.

Saturn achieved GM's primary objectives: Saturn was designed to help save General Motors by proving that GM could make a reliable vehicle. Period. Mission accomplished. It was an engineering success. It was a marketing success. And it was a sales success.

ALL PLANETS DIE

Life is change; things, people, company boards, politics – all change. In the end, GM violated our advice to them. They did *exactly opposite* of what we had time and time again recommended: they played up the GM tie to Saturn. And Saturn died. The death of Saturn was squarely on the hands of General Motors' leadership. They should have abided by the research.

As I see it, here is how it went down: After the first few years of healthy sales growth, GM parent branding gradually became more and more evident. The big move came in reaction to GM's cash crises due to the 2008 recession: financial people at GM made the decision to cut budgets for Saturn and go back to "badge engineering" in order to economize production. This is the old and stupid GM system in which several of vehicles (in this case Saturn branded vehicles) were also sold under other GM nameplates (in this case Pontiac). Dumb and short-sighted.

Badge-engineering: Trans Am and Camaro. Chevy and GMC trucks. It happens often, because it is cost-effective. But badge engineering does not work in all cases. And sometimes GM has decided not to badge-engineer: there is no badge engineering between Cadillac and any other division, leaving Cadillac as a one-off. GM had solid, well documented reasons to avoid that with Saturn, but they chose to ignore all that advice.

There had always been Saturn hate in the air at GM. For some GMers, Saturn was a rude rebuke of everything they had built and developed, and maybe in a few cases, of everything they lacked the courage to do.

What killed Saturn? The internal company politics surrounding the brand's very existence... and in that, GM's failure to strategically commit to Saturn's core meaning: a path of true differentiation. In the end, what killed Saturn was GM leadership's failure to strategically commit to the proper path.

In the end, Saturn's death was as inevitable as it was Shakespearean.

WHISKEY, CIGARETTES AND INDIANS

Coming off the Saturn project, I was in high demand at Landor. Egged on by some of Landor's biggest mouthpieces (our very effective business development specialists, our internal PR people and a few chief client officers) I toured key boardrooms at some of our biggest clients, talking about branding and positioning.

Suddenly everyone was paying much more attention to me than they ever had before. They were paying more attention to the things I said than I was myself. And that was scary. At first it seemed novel. Then I began to get a bit acrophobic about it all. I did lectures at Fortune 50 client retreats with audiences in the hundreds. I was on actual stages. At times my presentations were on screens 30 feet tall – an extreme rarity back in the 1980s. People listened to what I had to say (something I was not that used to, to tell the truth). I had people hanging on what I said and how I said it, way too much for my own comfort. It all seemed slightly insane.

After all, it was not like I was pronouncing elemental laws of the Universe. I was just talking about branding for chrissake. But people were taking this shit very seriously.

I had an extremely hard time with daily life. I was medicating to fall sleep, medicating to stay awake. I was eating terribly: road food, airport crap. And getting no exercise.

Then the inevitable happened: One night in Manhattan before a major presentation to a key client, I was having chest pains. I could not catch my breath. My heart was beating in a forceful, scary manner and I could not slow it down. I thought I was having a heart attack. I went to an ER, full of gun-shot victims and other limping, bandaged or bloody people. About five hours later I had not seen any doctors or nurses, and was still alive, so I left. I later figured out it was a full-fledged panic attack. It was another dark time, again.

My biggest supporters tended to be in two places: New York City and Europe, principally London. Some people seemed to just more easily embrace and understand branding back in those times. They seemed to be more humanistic and empathetic on the marketing spectrum. They understood at a gut level what I was talking about, and it is this:

People project. As humans we have a natural tendency to project and personify everything that we have a connection with, that we feel close to, even to impersonal or inanimate objects. Personification is something that as a species is natural to us. First, I think it is because we are herd animals. Second, I think that projection/personification is also a convenient (aka lazy) way to 'tag' objects and brands as good or neutral or bad.

We tend to personify those things with which we have the highest emotional feelings: guitars, guns, cars are all excellent examples. We 'tag' different companies and ascribe personalities and motives to them, far beyond reason. Not all brands get to be objects of projection, but some do. And when that happens, it helps to build the brand's worth.

So that's the core of the idea. Our Captain asked me to 'productize' what I had done with Saturn. A routine process of doing what we did. But for other clients. The first step was for me to develop a presentation, for such a program. We named it Brandworth, which we copyrighted as a service mark at the time.

My first client presentation of this concept and the process we used to bring it to life was given to Philip Morris executives at their annual marketing retreat in the late Spring of 1987 at the Greenbriar resort in West Virginia. My first two slides said that (1) products are made in factories and (2) brands are made in the consumer's mind. I made up those slides, myself. When I shared it with The Captain on the evening prior to our presentation at the Greenbriar, he flipped out. He loved it.

I was surprised to find when doing background research on this book that this thought is widely attributed personally to Walter Landor. And while I was fond of Walter, this may be a misattribution error. I suspect it is like Saturn being attributed to Roger Smith. I cannot find any hard evidence of this branding thought it being attributed to Walter, other than just hearsay or "cult of personality" marketing pieces written by the company many years later.

The fact is that it first appeared in my presentation to our biggest client in 1987. Hearing me say this, our chief client, and the key decision-maker CEO at Philip Morris (still alive so I will not mention him here) loved this thinking and our approach to building new brands. And we were almost immediately awarded two big branding projects as a result of this Greenbriar presentation.

TROPICAL VOODOO

I spent several weeks in Brazil with Philip Morris and its ad agency, doing qualitative research with indigenous people in Rio, Curitiba and Sao Paulo. Our mission was to understand brand positionings of various cigarettes, with the aim to developing a new brand for the indigenous peoples in Brazil. Yes, in the lens of today, this was many colors of "wrong." But in those days when about a third of the population smoked, and few really cared about cancer, it did not seem like what it does today.

Doing qualitative in a language other than your own is quite challenging. Making such an undertaking a bit more problematic in this instance, I spoke a little Spanish but not a word of Portuguese, the official language in Brazil. Within Philip Morris' office, this was not an issue; most people there were multi-cultural and spoke English fairly well. But beyond that it was a crapshoot. While Spanish and Portuguese are similar enough for me to navigate around a restaurant menu, it got dicey beyond that point.

So, to get around the language barrier, we hired an honest-to-God UN trained simultaneous translator to accompany us on the entire project.

There is no other way to frame this: watching this person in action was absolutely freaky. This translator listened to the interchange through headphones. Then as the conversation progressed, she interpreted the ongoing discussion word for word, in real time... and I mean in mere seconds after someone said something. It boggled my mind. How could this even be possible? How could a person do this? Her brain must have been wired differently than mine. This woman translated not only in the moment, but with the same inflections and intensity as those she was parroting. She even used different voices and hand movements to mirror the attitudes and inflections of the indigenous consumers.

All our focus group participants were white-shirted dark-skinned men. They seemed, as a culture, to like talking with their hands and arms. They habitually gesticulated wildly as they talked on the other side of the glass. She mirrored this, and more. It was quite the experience.

I felt like I was watching a magic show, or witnessing a special type of shape-shifter. The translator seemed utterly possessed. It was exhausting just to watch this sort of thing go on and on, for 90 minutes at a time. And after 90 minutes of this mental/temporal chaos, this United Nations-trained translator was drenched in perspiration; spent and exhausted. Her brain, understandably, required another 90 minutes of silence to reset. All completely relatable, and something that I have never witnessed before or since. I felt as though I was witnessing an experiment to plumb the absolute limits of the human brain. It felt almost extraterrestrial in its extreme difficulty. And she did this every day, for days on end.

On the last evening of the last focus group, we were in old Sao Paulo. We held these groups in an old mansion. Built in the 1900s, it looked to be right out of a Graham Greene spy novel. Centrally located and very old world, the antiquely decorated formal dining room had been functionally converted into a focus group facility with a one-way mirror. We sat in the observation room, and she listened in on the audio with a pair of headphones; her job was to translate as the discussion progressed.

After observing the first group, we all took a break. People filed out of our dark back-room chamber. Without saying anything, I noticed a small and silent interchange going on in the foyer between the other observers – people from the ad agency – and the receptionist. They would hand her their jewelry and valuables: rings, necklaces, ear rings and watches. She'd put the jewelry on a large metal ring. Then they'd leave. Over and over, I saw this. Wordless.

I approached her hoping she spoke English. "Why are people giving you their jewelry?" I asked.

She said it was because of the economy. Crime. She pointed at my crummy Casio watch, "That," she explained, "is worth a year's salary to many people." She explained that thieves cut off fingers to get rings. So, these days, everyone takes precautions; it is quite an automatic and unfortunate part of life now in this city with 1000% annual inflation.

I later learned that the entire Sao Paulo office of Leo Burnett Advertising had recently been invaded by men in masks carrying automatic weapons. Staffers were robbed of everything of any value: cash, jewelry, watches. In this city, with this run-way inflation, everyone felt in peril; everyone felt poor. With this ridiculous rate of inflation, everyone actually *was* poor. The head of the agency, in private, asked if me if we had any openings at Landor. It took my breath away.

I mean seriously: here we were, figuring out how to sell cigarettes to these struggling people? What the hell were we doing!? Why were we here? Why was I here? This is not right. I felt adrift, off-balance, and in such a strange land.

Our last group was commencing, so we all returned to our stations. It was yet another group of indigenous white-shirted, dark-skinned men, who by habit gesticulated wildly while sitting in this old-world dining room at its oval table. It was quite a pleasing spectacle. It felt like the Last Supper, but with animated, white-shirted, black-skinned participants.

Then, a mighty rainstorm came in, and took out the electricity.

The moderator's assistants brought in candles, and the center of the long table was filled with them, like an altar of sorts. The candles caught the white-shirted men's shadows, and in the flickering light, made their wild wigwagging gestures project onto the wood-paneled walls like that of storytellers in a cave in some ancient and forgotten world.

Since the power was out, we could not hear them even if we had wanted. So, to pass the time my translator talked about Makumba, the indigenous voodoo belief system, brought over with the slave trade in the 18th century from Africa. It is taken quite seriously by many in Brazil today, especially by the poor and disenfranchised. It is real voodoo. Some is white magic, and some is the other kind.

As they continued to talk and their shadows now played off the antique walls of this old candle-lit room, she told me that is is quite likely that these men here, they all practice Makumba voodoo, "That is why they all dress in this manner," she explained.

"Makumba is very powerful," she insisted as she lowered her posture and voice, talking secretly to me directly. "I myself believe in Makumba. I am a follower of this as well."

The candle light spectacle continued...

"In fact," she added, "I have been recently *cured* of the cancer. My priest took it right out of me, here," she pointed at her stomach, "through my navel, while I was in a trance just weeks ago." She leaned further, and with a deadpan serious expression and wide eyes slowly punctuated with almost a whisper now, she confessed, "It is all true."

I did not know what to say. The rain was making a deafening noise on the old house. The light: it seemed to change. Reflexively, and in ambiguity, I turned from her to look at the crowd in the antique room: the wild wigwagging gesticulations of the wiry white-shirted voodoo men and their wobbling shadows continued, boosted by the drafty dancing candlelight. And at that precise moment just about anything seemed possible in this hot, humid, tropical place.

The group ended. The rain continued. It was time for us all to go our separate ways. Perhaps forever.

So, we said our goodbyes. Handshakes and hugs. I desperately needed quietude. While several of them shared a taxi, I decided to walk back to my hotel through vacant and dark streets, in the oppressive, heavy monsoon rain.

Maybe the thieves are home asleep, I thought. Maybe Makumba will protect this foolish man.

With raindrops the size of quarters and soaked to the skin, I was numb from it all.

I have never been back to Brazil.

SHIPWRECK'D

I barely had time at home to catch my breath and unpack the crazy moments I had in Brazil. My next trip was to London to attend a client meeting with the people from our design group at our client United Rum Merchants. Trouble was, it was adjacent to my only child's first birthday. Naturally, I resisted going. I tried several times to decline, but in the end was told it was vitally necessary to the continued success of the relationship that I attend.

I honestly do not remember much of that meeting in London. I do remember that I was sort of the defensive lineman for Landor. They needed me there not because I had any expertise in design (I did not) but mostly because our team was a bit insecure. They were not up to the potential pressure that the client might put on us. But at the meeting, the client was kind, polite, and liked what we had to show them. In the end there was no pressure. Was it because I was there providing assurance? I'll never know. But I do know this: I glowered all the way home.

Over the weekend my wife and I celebrated our daughter's birthday by taking her to Marine World. She was only a year old... so of course she could not appreciate the difference between a whale and a windsock. A windsock would have been easier and cheaper and lasted longer. I guess the celebration was more for my wife and I, for successfully finishing a full year of parenting. And a lot more for her than for me.

A few days later I was still processing my feelings over having had to miss that real day. That day, I found out that one of the fellows I worked with was going through a hideous divorce – losing his wife, house and kids. I had never met his wife or kids. And I really did not know him all that well. To be honest about this, his pain – while terrible—was not really my pain. But this hit me hard because of how I felt about myself and my role as a husband and father. I was not there as much as I wanted to be, as much as she needed me to be. I didn't like myself these days.

I think we, collectively, were at a point where anything could have happened. I loved my wife and child with all my heart, and I was quite angry with the company and myself for the fact that I missed this milestone. The whole episode shined a light on fundamental priorities for me.

I had periodically been sucked into my job. The job was fascinating. And that was a good thing, right? It is nice to love what you do for a living. But the balance was all completely off. In the end the inescapable feeling was this: what you do for a living should complement—not compete with – the rest of your life. This gig, for all its amazing moments, was just not working.

Without question, the Landor chapter of my life had blown me away. It offered me the sorts of experiences and moments that stay with you throughout your life. It changed my life. And it was still going strong. I had met people and been in situations that I had never even realized were even possible. I'd been able to do things that I had never imagined, in places I never thought had existed in the world.

I thought of where I came from. This was a long way from the straight "D" grades of grammar school, the hand-me-downs and drug store jobs I'd held for economic necessity in high school. And the reality was that many of the guys I hung out with back then, were either dead or had done jail time. And here I was, living with the girl of my dreams, with a wonderful little baby at home, and in one of the coolest places on Earth: San Francisco. For a guy with a pretty marginal education, who wondered whether he'd even be alive at this point, it was all pretty great.

But still...

The very concept of 'work-life balance" had not yet been coined or, if it had, was certainly not in the zeitgeist. To the contrary, this was the era of the movie "Wall Street" and its central character Gordon Gekko. "Greed... is good!" he crowed. Gordon was a VCer. A corporate raider.

In flashbacks, I noticed that Gordon Gekko sounded just like the evil Ivy League cabal I had left in the dust at Arcata Corporation on Sand Hill Road in Menlo Park those years back.

In this time of glorified greed and corporate Darwinian imperatives, these more idealistic feelings I had were in the distinct minority. I struggled, and remember thinking that being forced to choose either family or job is just flat out wrong. You should be able to have both. And both seemed a good mission to go after.

So here I was, again at another damn fork in the road. This was a big decision coming, and I knew it. I had all this momentum built up and was capitalizing on it. But continuing down this road could – and possibly would – exact a horrible price: and a price I might pay for the rest of my life.

I felt like the moment was clear. The choice was fundamental. Just like that time I had to leave the street gang. It was a gang that had a different path, but a gang that had a life which was not mine to live, long term, a gang that would exact a price that was too steep.

And I knew that if I walked away from all of this right now that I would likely not ever have the fancy car, the big house, the Gordon Gekko trappings of material success. But I'd have my family and therefore my life. I hated the fact that it was an either/or. That I had to choose. But... I did.

There are moments in everyone's lives that are crucial pivot points. You get to a clear crossroads and through circumstance or situation, are given the chance to make a meaningful and important choice on your path.

And here I was. Stripping the Landor experience down, going beyond the limos and jet airplane rides, to the reality of what I was doing was the key. The ugly reality is that as fun and involving as it was, in the end *I was helping people sell whiskey and cigarettes to Indians. Literally.*

This was not the right path and we needed to change it dramatically.

So, like many moments previously... we set out to change everything. Again.

SIMPLY IMPOSSIBLE

My wife and I ascribed to the philosophy of Voluntary Simplicity, a philosophy which says essentially that sometimes a life with less complexity and outward material possessions can offer the space to be inwardly rich and that this is the better path. It was a Walden Pond sort of ideal, in which material possessions and big houses are not as important as peace and tranquility. Given my lifestyle in these times, it was some sort of psychological bulwark against the crazy high-pressured, three-piece-suited life that I was now living.

The conflict between what I was, and what I wanted had been there for a while, but lately with these current events, was grinding me down.

My goal, ever since college, had always been to live in "a small house in a cool place." This is what I had always told people when asked about my goals. And yes, in the Gordon Gekko era, I suppose that to some folks I came off like I was from Mars. But that was the ideal for me.

It was a dilemma: How many global marketing jobs are there in, say, a cool place like Lake Tahoe? Can a marketing consultant find a fit in a cool place like Moab, Utah? I could not work out how we could live in a cool place like that unless I was willing to start over, say, as a mechanic or painter or another tradesman. This sort of a profession, well it required a certain size of company, a critical mass that you just did not find out in the hinterlands. The way I was seeing things just then, perhaps in pursuing my research analyst career, I had inadvertently painted myself into a corner.

At the same time, I had always taken on my responsibilities to wife and child as a mission in life: to provide them with support, shelter, safety, opportunities for good health. I am not sure where that comes from, but it has always been at the deep core of who I am and what see as my duty. So, just taking a flier and finding a job as, say, a mechanic or unskilled laborer seemed to fly in the face of all that. It was a dilemma.

Then, I saw an ad in Ad Week from an ad agency in (of all things) Montana that needed a marketing/account executive. Having been raised in an advertising environment and done time as a scut worker in such a place, I knew that many if not most of my career skills could effectively transfer into that sort of a position. So, after talking it over with Ann and doing a bunch of secondary research, I applied for, interviewed at, and soon thereafter got the job at this smallish ad agency in the middle of nowhere, Montana. Bing-bam-boom. It was pretty much just that easy.

The hard part was about to begin.

My Landor co-worker/mentor Cowboy Bill absolutely loved Montana. He went there every summer to fly fish, and even had a Big Sky calendar on his office wall just above his computer. He talked about Montana a lot, sung its praises very often, and encouraged me to go there some day.

As we had been through a lot together, I had become his right-hand "go to" guy in many respects. With a feeling of loyalty, before talking to anyone else at Landor, I came in to tell him about my decision to leave.

"Bill, it's gotten out of control for me here, and so I've made the decision to leave. I got an offer from an ad agency."

"An ad agency? Are you serious?!?! After all I have told you about them?"

This hurt him; I knew that it would. This was more than abandonment; it was betrayal. So mad and hurt that he could not look at me, he stared at his happy place Montana wall calendar instead. Without looking at me he asked, "Where? Where are you going?"" He continued,

"You're looking at 'where,'" I continued, "It's an ad agency in Montana."

He turned; and looked; his mouth with a smile, his eyes sad, and looking a bit older and timeworn right then. His grin grew, with regret creeping in at the corner. His eyes a little watery... he smiled and said, "Well, godddddamn, Sundance! I guess you've gone and done it now."

We were parting ways. These are the moments in life – the ones when you leave people behind – which gnaw at me still. When you leave and it becomes a final, forever sort of thing. You never admit it, you never quite say goodbye, but instead, say "see you later." You know that time will go on, and that it is likely your relationship will not. Oh, you might keep in touch. But it will be different, and never the same again. "Never" just plain hurts. Time is heartless and cruel that way.

They threw me a party. The artists made me a huge card all about Arcadian fields and noble intent. They all so well understood why I was doing this thing. They all wished me success and pleasant journeys, every one of them. So we packed up the house, loaded the car and set off for greener pastures.

As we pulled away from our rental house in the beautiful hills of the East Bay, U2 was on the car radio. "And I still haven't found what I'm looking for..." Words were never sung as true.

CHAPTER V: HELL IS MT

"Hell is empty,

All the devils are here."

- William Shakespeare

I never lived in the Montana you see on television. That Montana does not exist. Frankly, that Montana has never totally existed in any real, sustainable manner. There are islands of the posterized, ideal Montana, but for the most part that construct really only exists for tourists. Even further from that misty-eyed fantasy, we went to a place that in the end felt culturally more akin to Oklahoma or North Dakota than to the mountain-and-stream paradise that most conjure up in their minds when they think of Montana.

I went to a small ad agency in a place ironically called Great Falls, a remarkably uninspired city of 60,000 souls. First, it was not "great" at all. It was a place of 60,000 people and had one mall, and one movie theater. The "great falls" along the Missouri River had long since been dammed over to create power. The mountains? They were an about hour's drive in any direction. They held a moderate amount of interesting terrain, but much of it was locked up making for access problems as they were usually surrounded by working cattle ranches.

This ad agency had all the big and most conservative (and stable) clients including the power company, the state travel account, and several large and lucrative divisions (ag and private banking) for a large and revered financial institution as its anchor clients. It had momentum, money and was stable and growing. The leadership had expanded to nearby Spokane, Washington, and since that had gone well, had plans to grow again by acquisition, into Boise or Salt Lake City. This growth and stability, together with the reasonable possibility that I could lead a new satellite of this agency, were the draw.

Lewis Frank was the key shareholder, major cheerleader, morale booster, business getter, deer hunter and picnic chef. It was one of those ad agencies which took over an uninspired accounting firm's office, and did the best they could to jazz the place up while spending close to zero dollars on the project. Lewis was natural promoter and a shrewd businessman.

Lew could have been, in another life a small-town newspaper guy, a Friday Night Lights sports radio reporter, a horse breeder, or even an antique dealer with a penchant for casino life. Or all of those rolled into one.

He tended to wear checked sports coats, a pork-pie hat and had an accent that might have been Iowan, or Wisconsinite in origin. He talked in headlines. Big bold sentences. Sharp, and just a little nasal. He was in his 60s, but fit, quick and was the sort who actually might be counted on to say things like "Get off my Lawn." And I am sure he had the shotgun to go with that image. He was, in short, a bona fide character of the first degree.

One day, while barreling down the highway in his bouncy and noisy Landcruiser, out of the blue he shouted, "Rod, do you like wood?!?"

Now here's the thing: We had absolutely not been talking about wood. Like, ever. Moreover, we had not even *seen* wood. Driving across the tundra, there was by definition *zero wood* in eyesight. Right, left, ahead, behind. Zero wood. So, you can understand my weird carnival of emotions and all the possible torrent of snarky reactions I imagined, upon hearing this question. My mind was a wheel of fortune of reaction models: Amusement. Confusion. Fear. Definite puzzlement. I had no friggin' idea what to say.

He continued, "I like wood! I like *looking at it*! I like *chopping* it! I like *burning* it! Ahh, the *smell* of burning wood! I like *everything* about it! I LIKE wood, Rod!" he concluded.

Silence.

This was Lew. And as I would discover, classic Lew. Where the wood observation came from? Where it went? Why that exclamation even ever existed? Who the hell knows? Who would ever know? As unknowable as the mysteries of the Sphinx. Still, this was the guy:

the head of this little ad agency in the middle of Montana. I honestly cannot remember what happened next. I am sure something did, but that part is just gone. But the point is, that is who this guy was. A strange guy for sure. And one in a million.

One of our clients ... and one of the reasons I felt this ad agency was for real, was this very large banking firm that is famous across the West, still to this day. They put me on a part of this business early in my tenure there, to see what I could do in getting in good, and in growing the business. After having visited bank managers in about 20 towns all across rural North and South Dakota (itself an educational journey), I had a one-on-one lunch in Minneapolis with the lead marketing guy; the same one who would in time become the Chairman of the Board of this banking system. A little older than me, he was closer to my generation than Lew's, and we got on well enough. About midway through our pleasant lunch the focus turned to Lew. And mister future Chairman leaned in and conspiratorially asked, "So, level with me here: is Lew for real? I mean, with his checkered sport coats and hat and everything, is he just putting everybody on? He seems like a character or something... like he is from another time."

He was. And so was most of Montana.

I think I realized at that early point that yep, this is an odd ad agency, in an equally odd place. And the entire reason that this ad agency even exists in the first place is largely because it is the only reliable option in this weird, cowboyed and frozen hell of a tundra wasteland. This ad agency had the business it did because we, unlike any other agency, claimed to know how to talk to their clientele – mostly cowboy ranchers in Montana, Wyoming and the Dakotas. And this much is true: we did know how to talk to them, and boy, they were of a different cut back then.

I wondered how long I would last in this frozen frontier hell, right at that moment.

Lew and his wife had bought the agency for a song, and then built this business up, providing a place for people who had "advertising-ish" talents to hone their craft. To be sure, a few of the people at this agency were more talented than others. One or two were genuinely good at their jobs. But to be honest, there were also quite a few people who really had no place in advertising, and deep down, they fearfully knew this about themselves. They were the ones to give a wide berth. Like animals in the jungle, the insecure ones always prove to be the most dangerous.

I remember befriending a hippy couple and going to a party at their place, full of people in their 20s and 30s, most of whom were college educated. In a group of guys, I asked for a show of hands on how many hunted and fished. Seven of ten hunted, ten of ten fished. This was what one did up there. This was everyone's pastime. What the hell else was there to do here?

Montana in the early 1990s was an odd place full of cowboys, wanna-be cowboys and cows. Some wheat farmers and Hutterites too. Once a year the ranchers and wanna-be's would tend to get all mushy about First Nation folks, but other than that, the Native Americans were expected to stay on the rez.

The wilderness areas were mostly locked out by the ranchers who owned the spreads just outside the wilderness areas. Heck, it was not their fault. It's not like they said, "Hey let's buy up all this land next to the protected areas just to mess with the hikers." So, there was not much day hiking.

And if you went hiking, you had better bring a gun. Most folks who hiked were carrying 357 magnums, or colt 45s. For bear protection, because there were grizzlies all over the place. Especially up along the Rocky Mountain front in proximity to Glacier National Park. The talk at the time was that the bears near Yellowstone had aversion training, and learned to stay away from humans. But up at Glacier, it was the reverse. It was the humans who had learned to stay away from bears. And up there, the bears looked for humans actively. So, you brought a gun. And if you did not, you felt incredibly vulnerable.

In Montana everybody was suspicious of the government. It really didn't matter much which government. And the power company. Again, didn't matter which one. People really did ascribe to the ethic of rugged individualism and letting people be whatever they wanted. And in leaving everyone be. It was interpersonal detente on a grand scale. The core ethos in Montana was all about personal liberty, and the attitude was, "Just as long as yours does not interfere with mine, go ahead and do your thing and I'll do mine."

We (my wife, infant daughter and I) were regarded as an immigrant family, and treated as such. Fresh off the boat, except we were fresh off the jet plane. Just like the 'big city person goes to the sticks' TV shows, people did, in fact, sort of have it in for us. People were betting on our failure to tough it out there. They hated outsiders, especially Californians. And yes, we constantly were the object of small aggressions, sabotage and social shunning. But we kept on. We were much more stubborn back then.

My first "field trip" assignment was to go to a bull auction someplace along the front range of the Rockies (the mountains West of us), to a ranch just south-southeast of the Blackfeet Rez. I was told that a white guy didn't want to be caught there alone. As it was a stone's throw from an area called a "fen," especially favored by grizzly bears for all its forage, it seemed like it was a place that – heck—nobody ever wanted to be caught alone.

As one may recall, while doing my Landor thing, I had morphed from a hippy hiker to a suit-and-wingtips wearing professional. And because I had only been in Montana a few weeks, my outfit on this day was no exception. I was suited up, and clad in my black dress shoes. The further I got into the foothills of the Rockies, the more uncomfortable I felt about my wardrobe choices of the day. By the time I got to the ranch, I was feeling mighty out of place.

Roundup Ranch, as we'll call it, was pure Montana: Rusty trucks, beat up trailers to haul livestock, and cowboys. Lots of them. Old ones, mostly. Ranch foremen, owners, each one all dusty and leathered. Everybody looked like people who work outside year-round for a living. In Montana. And here I was, mister wingtips. Man, oh man.

Most of the area was mud, once-mud or soon-to-be mud that had dried into peaks and gullies roughly conforming to cattle hoofs or post holes. The dry spots would soon be mud again. This constituted a moderately challenging path to walk in my now shit-and-mud-encrusted dress shoes. I hobbled along, following the crowd of guys in big hats, filing through a wide door into an old-looking wooden building.

The auction took place in an old, unadorned, unpainted and more or less circular wooden building. The crowd slowly filed into this dimly lit wooden cavern and climbed into the creaky bleachers around its periphery. Think the Globe Theater, but ringed in bull excrement and transported into the Old West.

This was an enclosed arena with ceilings that were maybe 40 feet high. The wooden bleachers were curved and carved to match up with the walls all around three quarters of the interior of the structure. Just there, on the one open quarter with no bleachers was a raised auctioneers stand, flanked by two barn doors on either side of the auction stage. Bulls could be seen lined up in the left-hand door, most being held by ropes affixed to ring noses by leathery stoic-looking men who were ready to bring them into the ring, one at a time, to be evaluated by the assembled ranchers. This seemed a moment and a scene that has not changed much on a hundred years, maybe several hundred or even a thousand years, in some places on earth. It took my breath away.

Amazed at the timelessness, I waited in suspense. I paid more attention to what was about to happen in this event than to the very occasional eye-rolls and or small smirks leveled at my greenhorn attire and shit-encrusted, wholly inappropriate footwear. For the most part, cowboys seemed to have a world-worn live and let live way about them here in Montana. And that is something which I suspect is true to this day.

Then it started: Bulls were led in one by one; measurements were made of all their essential parts, announced to the crowd, and bidding commenced. The auctioneer was a professional like one might hear in the movies. Hard to follow and sometimes lightening quick, each bull auction lasted about three to five minutes. After about 30 minutes, I began to be able to roughly anticipate the ultimate price paid for each bull.

How big the world is. I was a stranger in a strange land. Even an antique land. This was living; this was participant observation in its finest form. For all its strangeness it could have been a Trobriand Islander ritual, or a Druid Moon Dance. A Mummers ritual from the

Middle Ages. It was fascinating: at once both alien and familiar. I learned a lot about Montana that afternoon, and also a little about choosing my wardrobe accents to be more situationally appropriate.

The arc of life. Cultural whiplash. Put any of these cowboys in those big city situations full of limos and jets, why they'd feel just as weird as I do, here and now in this bull pen. Everything's relative.

After about a month of working at the agency the people there began to be more at ease with my meeting of, and interacting with actual clients. And as the veil of the new job lifted, it became obvious that my core client was to be the Montana Power Company. One morning, I accompanied Lew's wife, one of the agency's senior people, to meet the key Montana Power people in Butte, Montana.

Getting to Butte involved a drive of two and a half hours and crossing two mountain ranges. Butte itself is an old mining town and has as its dominant feature, a deep pit full of toxicity that measures 1 mile by ½ mile. It's still an EPA superfund site. That saying, Butte is far from a garden spot. While $48 billion worth of copper was extracted from these mines, very little ever stayed in Butte for long.

When we got to Montana Power, we met with the two fellows that interfaced with the ad agency. Both worked on the communications team, came from journalism backgrounds and were classically trained writers... quite technically excellent writers, in my opinion. We met in a small conference room at first, and then later I accompanied the more junior of the two – my primary contact going forward—to his cubicle/work area. In order to keep my lawyers happy, we'll call him Udo.

Udo was of Basque heritage; dark skinned, heavyset, wild haired and had a sort of trashy and remarkably ill-trimmed moustache. It was the kind of moustache that almost had a life of its own, the way it would misalign with his features however it felt most appropriate. Other than this mustache, the other curious thing about Udo upon meeting him was that his eyes were not aligned... By that I mean that one eye tracked one way, the other eye beat to a different drummer. Both eyes worked and he could see perfectly well out of either. They just did not happen to be aimed at the same thing at the same time. He used this to his advantage, keeping everyone a little unsure and off balance, guessing about what he was looking at, or even meaning. If the eyes are a window to the soul, this guy's soul was a bit wacky and hard to predict.

The combination of his unpredictable moustache and his unusual eyes gave him an almost chronically insane appearance most of the time. I suspect that living in this old mining town, he was one of the "local color" people when out on the streets.

He occupied a cubicle toward the outside of their department's area. His oversized workstation featured a large, wrap-around desk, a credenza, several shelves and a computer and keyboard. But oddly, I noticed that I could not actually *see* any of the surfaces. No. They were buried deep (actually inches deep) below an undulating mass of papers, magazines, letters, and binders. It was mesmerizing... almost topographic. It heaved from one hill rolling into the next: impressive in a certain way. The guest chair in his cubicle was similarly buried under layers of this terraform. He instructed me to clear a place to sit on the guest chair by moving "that stack there" (a sort of topsy pile of miscellany) to the floor next to the chair. The area directly under the chair had already been occupied in some previous paper relocation endeavor by an earlier guest, at one time or another.

I got to know Udo gradually, incrementally. Over time I found that he was one of those people who seemed to delight in finding the snarliest and most aggressive way possible to get his point across.

Almost like Supervisor Candace from Chicago, I thought. But there was a key difference here. After being his bellicose self, he almost always backpedaled like an abusive spouse might, in order to dress the inflicted wounds so that if pressed, he could be seen, and perhaps also see himself as being 'nice.' This made working with him feel endlessly punitive and painful most of the time.

But nobody is black-and-white and Udo also had courage. This is quite functional in advertising. He specifically had a compass of sorts, and had the courage to do what he felt was right within the organization. He did not hesitate to go against the grain and fight for what he found to be the Just Cause. And so, this factor, in the mix with his less admirable qualities, proved to count for much through our otherwise horrible relationship.

The fact of the matter was that this extremely risk adverse public utility in Montana desperately needed bold action if it was ever to be taken seriously by the public. In this situation, Udo's courage was valuable. He and he alone was willing to push the bureaucracy at Montana Power in that necessary direction. This proved to be his (only) redeeming quality in the end.

Classified as a 'carpetbagger from California," Udo made it clear that I did not know Montana, or Montanans. He told me I did not know writing like he did. And so Udo made it his duty to micro-manage every ad we developed. He rewrote all the copy. Sometimes we went through as many as ten revisions on a single idiotic print ad, going back and forth so fast that he often criticizing me for copy that *he had in fact originally written*. He also dictated the often cliché visuals. And the result were ads that had no spark, lacked focus, seemed cloying, heavy-handed, and lame. Some ads included, by his hand, every copy point ever imagined and became laundry lists of boredom. All were lacking any cohesive strategy, look or feel. The work was terrible. And he, as their author, was the client from hell.

And the result of all this attempted advertising? Embarrassment and low morale on our end, and wasted money from the client. And zero response from consumers. We were putting out a series of terrible, dull, unimaginative crap.

Maybe the best thing is that the ads were so bad that people did not look at them. We achieved absolutely zero business results. Consumers kept on distrusting the utility as much as they did the government. And we were putting out a lousy and ineffectual product.

Everyone on the team felt bad. All the people at the agency blamed me. They hated me for not "being better" at managing my client. And what could I do? I was no more able to manage Udo than a crew of fire fighters could manage an inferno. In hell.

Times were tough. It was now January—the frigid middle of the Montana winter. Gray skies. Too much snow. Lots of ice. Cars that had to be plugged in so that the oil would not freeze. We had 30 below Fahrenheit temperatures for weeks on end. Dull skies. My wife and I were both cranky from the lack of sunlight and warmth. Our daughter was teething and cranky. I was shunned socially; I had no friends at the agency. The client seemed to openly despise me. These were desperate times. And the global life I had once at Landor? It seemed like a distant planet in a made-up Universe.

Due to Udo's dictates and pugilistic manner, we ran through two copywriters and two art directors in as many months. On one dim and ice-fogged Tuesday, in the middle of this bone-breaking Montana winter, on my now lonely, dark and cold lunch hour, I parked my Jeep in an empty parking lot along the Missouri river.

I thought. I thought about the life we had left. I thought about this desperately cold and hopeless situation. Mostly I thought about this perilous predicament that I had placed my family in. The guilt overwhelmed me. And for the first time in many years, I broke down in this mile-deep sadness. I cried.

I was utterly defeated. Failed. Without hope. Ashamed. What had we done? What had *I* done? I had bought the brochure, not the reality. I had moved my family to this bleak and ice-locked place. I... me. I had let *everyone* down. I thought about the management people at this agency. I had been played: *they* knew this horrible guy; *they* hired me because I was ignorant, and because nobody else would take this account. *They* absolutely knew this would happen. *They* saw this coming. I had been *totally taken* by these sneaky people. I was expendable. I had wholly been hoodwinked by these horrible people in whom I had placed my trust... into taking over this absolutely terrible client. What were they thinking? How could they have been so evil and manipulative? I was trapped. In this hell hole, in this endless Montana winter. I was angry.

Hell is MT, all the devils are here.

The Missouri River was actually, literally, frozen over. I never thought that was possible. But in this weather of temperatures that plummeted to -20 and -30 for weeks on end, anything was possible. I sat there in my Jeep Cherokee, watching the stillness through the ice fog. Panic was not far from my mind. The flush of sorrow and sadness and hopelessness and anger was overwhelming.

Another long shot in my string of long shots. Like breaking from the street gang back in Chicago, I had leapt – this time to Montana. Only this time I had unwittingly been pushed into this suicide mission that others surely had seen as hopeless. It seemed impossible. A mission doomed to failure. That's why they hired me, the bastards.

Oh sure, I had built up some confidence over the years in my ability to overcome lots of difficult client situations. But this? This seemed impossible. My position seemed hopeless. Getting out of Montana? I mean in what fantasy would that ever happen? What was I to do? What *could* I do?

I pulled myself together. I had to. While I wanted to flee for the hills, there was really no choice but to go on. I went back to the office, like a good soldier to my post. Once there, I avoided even making eye contact with anyone, lest I go volcanic and punch one of these assholes at the ad agency. So, I power walked in, head down, and closed the door to my office.

I spent the next few hours drinking coffee and just plain staring at the work, all taped to six-foot-tall sheets of foam core, leaning against my office walls. I looked at the 'feedback' from the client... piles and piles of copy marked up in red, with long lines of micro-mangled bullshit copy, terribly hackneyed turns of phrase from Udo. Idiotic visuals that made no sense. It was all utter crap. But it was crap that he paid for and made us run in the media.

The work product was all so very embarrassing. I decided that Udo needed to see what I was seeing. Go big or go home: I made a "portfolio" to hold all the work loose leaf style, and then I photoshopped a cut-out of a toilet seat lid for the portfolio cover. Then I compiled all the client-made, client-written, client-dictated junk that this was, got in my Jeep, and made the 120+ mile trip across two snowy, bleak and ice-locked mountain ranges to see him.

Finally, in a conference room I presented his own blessed crap in the toilet bowl. I made the point that this was not helping him, his company or the public. That things needed to change. Big change.

Pause.

True to form, Udo shot back and said, "You're right, this is total crap. Your agency is giving us crap. It's all your fault. You need to fix this. Either get me breakthrough creative, or we'll take our business elsewhere. You have 30 days to show me something great."

Smooth move, idiot. Hoisted on my own petard. Except it was the petard he made all by himself and despite our best efforts to the contrary. And now my petard again. These days we would call it "gaslighting." But there I was, whatever the correct term. My mission was clear: either strangle him right now in this very room, or develop a really killer campaign. So I went with the campaign.

This was my final challenge... and I realized it might be the hill that I would die on. The campaign's goal was to get people to convert from woodstoves to natural gas for home heating. As bizarre as it sounds, despite this incredibly cold winter environment of 30-below extremes in Montana, a very large number of people still used wood (stoves and fireplaces) to heat their homes. Frontier cowboy culture. The particulate pollution was quite hazardous to health, and choking out the big sky in our Big Sky state. The haze was especially serious in the valleys of Western Montana. We needed these cowboys to abandon their wood fires and convert to natural gas. Piece of cake...

On the road back home, I had a lot of time to think, ponder, let my mind wander. Driving longer distances has always been good for that. That late afternoon, coming out of the Missouri River canyon and into high open rolling grasslands between me and the next dark mountain range I witnessed something that I sorely needed at that moment: against a background of snowy peaks, I stopped when I saw a herd of about 70 or more pronghorn antelope, running down one grass-and-snow covered hill, then disappearing, rising again on the far hill, only to disappear over that crest again. Free, leaping and galloping pronghorn. This was a spectacle I had never expected and totally needed at this moment. It was a reset of the highest order.

I went back to the agency, got a new copywriter assigned to the account and talked the associate creative director, Evan, into coming onto the special project team, as I was calling this.

We tried and tried and tried to come up with creative. We spent a week just spinning our wheels. Even though I was not supposed to be in on creative meetings, I joined since my future and that of my family were pretty much on the line at the time. Nothing was hitting solidly. I was getting desperate, thinking we were doomed.

Some background here: I deeply love my family. I changed my life for them in moving to Montana, and would change it again and again without blinking; without question. In Montana, I could go home every day and eat PB&J sandwiches with my little girl. Every single and wonderful day. This is part of what I signed up for. I was a very engaged dad, and used to play Legos and Playmobile with my daughter quite a bit. I made her a mountain valley out of paper mâché where she could develop her worlds of play. An only child, it was an important part of her young life, especially in the long Montana winter. As a part of our playtimes, we'd use our imaginations to personify inanimate objects a lot. As it turns out, this is what saved us all.

As stated, the advertising goal was to come up with an engaging way to talk about switching from woodstoves to natural gas in order to clean up the smokey skies of Big Sky country. One day in our war room, staring at all our not-quite-great-ideas on the wall, I thought about my daughter and how we personify things when we play... it hit me like a bolt from the blue I blurted out "let's personify wood stoves as evil."

We developed a series of three hilarious and compelling TV spots doing just that. Each pulled the viewer into the moment: a woman talking about her lying and unreliable partner who filled her with "empty promises;" a man berating a messy irresponsible teen that smokes; another dealing with a recidivist criminal/friend who talked big but messed things up every time. In the last part of each ad, we revealed that the object of ire was not a person, but instead a woodstove. Then we followed with the call to action. These ads were arresting, funny, and had high filmic production value. They worked hard and well.

And then the impossible happened: Udo loved them. Then the unexpected part: in his enthusiasm he barely changed a word of copy! We produced, aired and prayed a bit... then we measured the results. The public loved it. The natural gas partners in the construction trades did too. We saved the account, my family's future, and what remained of my sanity. This successful campaign raised my cred with Udo, and his manner became much easier to endure.

We continued down this path with Udo for another several years, doing three separate, highly memorable, results-producing and even nationally award-winning campaigns. Each one was a little more outrageous than the next. And Udo grew more trusting and less dictatorial. We did spots parodying a popular and quite surreal TV series, we produced another series that had a Sci-Fi story full of plot twists dealing with aliens, and ads that poked fun at life. They all worked. They all brought results, won awards and even generated controversy within Montana Power Company. All good things.

And then the inevitable happened: entropy. Entropy rules the Universe, and everything – every damn thing – breaks at some point. Someone on the team – someone who I did not like, did not interact with, but unfortunately had a bigger mouth than he did common sense... said and did something politically disastrous. Unforgivable. Then laid it at the collective agency's feet. It created a PR situation for the company and ruined the trust of the client team. In the end it was dumb, excusable and frankly quite petty. But it opened the door to one of our very hungry competitors to come into the picture, and the account just slid away.

This illustrates agency life, and why it is as perilous as life can be. Your death is coming; it is just a matter of when and where. And usually, just like in my prophesized Early Demise Hypothesis, you do *not* see it coming in advance.

LAST GLIMPSE OF THE WILD

During this time our try-hard little ad agency had other victories. Among other things I got involved in the winter sports group coordinating all state-funded tourism promotion. Having been a skier, this was more fun than I felt was legal for a time. I got to hang out with a lot of the ski area operators, guide services and National Park concession teams. It was a fine time.

I had to alter my presentation style a bit. Far from the Fortune 50 audiences of 100+ people sitting in cascading tiers of crushed velvet chairs, my venues were somewhat less formal. One day: a hallway in a ski locker room. The next day: a greasy spoon diner talking to an assortment of outfitters, wranglers, and backcountry guides about advertising and marketing programs that were designed to help them economically.

This gig was the most absurd. They: just off the trails from milking cows or fixing fences, or whatever the hell it is they do out there. Me: a representative from the government. My message: "Hi, I am from the government and I am here to help." They mostly looked at me like I was from Mars. Even I had a hard time keeping a straight face. But still, I tried to help them and help their businesses. It kept me honest about the diversity of people in the world.

The evening before the Lincoln, Montana meeting, was during a cold week in late October. I was staying in a little one room cabin that would ordinarily be seen as "cute" by the tourists. For me it was just small and cold. I went across the road (the highway ran through the almost invisible little town) and got some take-out fried chicken. It was dark and snowing pretty heavily – the fluffy snow that accumulates and muffles everything. There was only one single solitary street light on each end of this 2-block town. The roads and stores were abandoned to the snow. There was nobody around. Crossing the wet, dark and empty main drag, as I got to the mid-point of the road I saw some movement through the gloom to my right: a doe about 50 years away headed the opposite direction from me, barely lit from the misty, rosy lights of the restaurant sign, and faintly silhouetted by the distant street light.

We each froze for a second, exchanging gazes. And after a beat, we each continued on our separate ways in the silence of the snow. There and gone and there forever, frozen in time, a signature moment in the Montana chapter.

What a different experience this was from Landor Associates. I stayed engaged with this agency to a point. But my end came when I realized that they were not, as they had once told me, going to acquire another agency in either Boise or Salt Lake City. I had been involved in negotiations on both; but both talks had broken down in deadlocks over cash. Lewis became fatigued. He had a few health problems. Then, Lew retired and sold his interests to the wrong folks. Some clients left, turned off by repeated incomptence and rumors of what some people said were alleged off-book dealings or campaign contributions to politicians in hopes that this would influence much of the State businesses that we now handled. Just rumors, but rumors do damage. It was, once again, a dark time.

By way of recommendation by a friend, I was approached by a film production company. The owner had been jilted by her now former husband who owned an ad agency. She wanted blood. Her plan: financially underwrite a new ad agency in order to financially ruin him. So, she hired me and another fellow to do the dirty work of going after his clients and destroying his business.

It was born in evil intent, but it was all I could do at the time. It just stunned me at how constitutionally horrible so many people could be to so many others. But it was the best option of many horrible options... I was hoping to turn coal into diamonds. Hoping I could make something better of our lives in the process.

The fellow I was shackeled to in this initially evil enterprise we will call Reginald. Reginald had been a creative director at many agencies, and somehow found himself here, in Montana. The reason? He was insufferable. More than quite full of himself, he defined vainglorious. He once told me about how he had been listening to something – Beethoven, I think – and began to cry. Not out of the beauty of the music, or how it still touched people hundreds of years after its composition. Not for the talent of the musicians who had devoted their lives to learning these difficult pieces. Not for the society that had honored this beautiful music universally, kept it and celebrated it. Instead, he cried because he realized how fortunate he was to be singularly intellllgent enough to fully appreaciate all the sublties of the composition. He cried for the grandeur of his own brain, the damn narcissist. Insufferable.

Reginald was from the South, had a sort of dilitantish air about him, sported what he thought was an "ironic" moustache and had a love of brimmed hats. Avodado-shaped, he was more of a grenenhorn than I had ever been. To the delighted derision of his neighbors, he had a burro and rode it around his "ranch," actually a worthless tract of scrub land up on the wind-swept and barren plains between Great Falls and the Front Range. An ass upon an ass, if there ever was one.

When I joined up with this outfit, Reginald was already at work on our first ad program, aimed at motivating women to avoid smoking during pregnancy. The ad he produced featured the lullaby "rock-a-bye baby." To the beat of this tune, the viewer saw nails being hammered into wood. As the camera pulled back, the camera revealed that the nails were going into the lid of an infant-sized coffin. The final screen was that of an expectant mother in a rocking chair, smoking a cigarette. The whole ad was devastating in an unblinking and shocking way. The ad was pulled the same day that it aired. A woman had attempted suicide after seeing the ad. Her baby was stillborn just weeks earlier.

Reginald was proud of this work.

Seeing the deep monstrosity of the real Reginald, I suggested that we needed another good creative person to be added to the team in order to give Reginald more freedom. I leaned on a very creative friend (and former associate creative director) from the earlier ad agency, and asked him to join us.

In a few months, and with some difficulty, the two of us successfully parted ways with Reginald. We also parted ways with the opinionated, suffocating and jilted owner of the production company. This left us with less "evil" but also less working capital. But it gave us the freedom to do whatever we wanted to do.

My partner (we'll call Ryan) was a friend and close comrade. He was a renaissance guy if there ever was one. It seemed like there was no musical instrument he could not master, and aside from being our creative powerhouse, was in usually no less than two different bands at any one time (sometimes three). And he was good, I mean really soulful s a musical artist, and technically good to boot. He was also much more of a people person than I, and his gregariousness won us a lot of new business. People just loved him.

It was a scary time. Montana was not an economic epicenter of ad spending, and so we had to get creative with what we did and who we worked with. We had a regional bank, courtesy of my partners connections. We took on any potential clients that we could find.

One day we got a call from an inventor who wanted to market a new technology that he had patented which could boil an egg in five seconds. He needed marketing and advertising assistance, and it seemed that we could really help him. His technology, he continued, would have both industrial as well as commercial potential, aside from the energy savings. We arranged for him to come into the office for a meeting. He was excited to show us the technology and discuss how we might market it.

A few days later, he arrived. About six feet five, he was a rail thin fellow with white tussled hair, who seemed to have a look of perpetual surprise on his face. We ushered him into the conference room whereupon he got to the business of setting up his "equipment" to demonstrate the technology to us.

When finished, we filed in: me, Ryan, and our hyper-organized and extremely competent account assistant May. There on the table was a basket of eggs, a small soup bowl, and a device that looked like a Bunsen burner base, with a six-inch long needle in place of the flame. The whole assembly was electrified in some fashion, and plugged into our wall socket.

"This," he explained, "is the El-Egg-trocutor. Harmless when touched, it can hard boil an egg in under ten seconds."

He took one of the eggs in the basket, broke it into the bowl to demonstrate, as would a magician, that these were in fact raw eggs.

"Now, I will hard boil an egg by impaling it on the electric needle." He said theatrically, as he confidently placed it on the needle.

There was a momentary hum, and then without any more fanfare, the egg exploded with a loud POP. There was raw-ish egg and bits of eggshell everywhere. All over the walls, our clothing, our faces. Everything.

While I think we all were rooting for him, like in a Saturday Night Live sketch, we all were sort of waiting for something to go awry. This was, of course, more spectacular a finish than I had imagined! We all tried so very hard not to laugh, but it was sort of an impossible struggle.

He wiped some egg off his face and tousled hair and mumbled with a shrug, "This has only happened a few times before," and apologized.

We felt bad for the poor guy, and worried about the health effects of getting raw egg in our eyes, etc. He left, and (not surprisingly) never came back. It took a lot of careful cleaning to get the egg off the grass-cloth wallpaper in our conference room.

Such was life as a streetside ad guy in our wild West.

Some clients were bigger than that, thankfully. My favorite client was T.W. Recreational Services. They leased and operated all the hotels within Yellowstone National Park.

We did print pieces for them: magazine ads, maps, brochures, rack cards and things of that nature. Our job involved researching the all the park, its lodging and recreational facilities and attractions, and then create all the materials. Best of all it was my job to source all the photos and footage that were necessary for the different pieces. Most of the photographers down there worked either for the park as rangers, or in various jobs for the concessionaires. Some lived in or near the park year-round – not an easy thing to do in a place that got up to ten feet of snow, had bison the size of cars and marauding grizzlies the rest of the time. One photographer had, as his winter job, the duty of scaling to the roofs of the lodges and – using a crosscut timber saw – carving the snow into tall pillars and then sliding them off the roofs so that the snow did not collapse the roofs under their weight.

My contacts (clients and suppliers) were for the most part really colorful folks, the sorts of people who came right out of storybooks. They were many of today's real mountain folks and fully looked the part. This group of park employee/creative types were a interesting bunch, and this wonderful and enriching experience allowed me to relate to and understand the mindsets of people who, in a different life, I would never in a million years have even seen, let alone known as individuals.

We spent time in and around Livingston, Montana which at the time was a small and uncrowded place in which a lot of the people in town knew one another on a first name basis. Back in those days it did not seem like many tourists came into Livingston. We went to the Livingston Rodeo over one July 4 weekend, and sat in the vacant corner of the spectator stands. We befriended a Hutterite boy who was also sitting up there. I think we started our conversation because he seemed hot and we had extra waters and treats. It turned out that he had hated living in the colony and spent as much time as he was able away from them and their influences. He wore classic Hutterite attire, but he sure seemed to like cowboying quite a bit. He seemed destined to run away to a working ranch one day, and become a ranch hand, much as you might imagine from some popular TV show. Still today I think of that boy, and wonder what became of him.

This was the true west, and something that we were able to experience in the course of our daily lives. It almost became ordinary, but thankfully never did totally.

We (my wife, daughter and I) would routinely stay at an old turn-of-the-century hot springs resort located off the highway on the park's northern access road. It was a creaky old place, built some time ago. It looked and felt exactly right for the region. It had, as one of its many features, a huge lawn with a very long and shaded porch, outfitted with many rocking chairs. Children would play in the meadow, while we adults would sit in the rockers, contentedly sipping our afternoon libations. It was a fine way to end any day in the Paradise Valley.

One particular day I happened to note that my daughter had found a nice friend to play with. Something amusing happened with the kids, and I glance off to my left to see if the other parents had noticed, if only to exchange smiles and nods. And somewhere in that gaggle was Peter Fonda. We all shared a smile and went back to our business. He lived nearby, as did his sister Jane and her new boyfriend Ted Turner. I was a bit taken aback that they would be here, at this Hot Springs, given their celebrity and resources. Perhaps it was just for this: the simple pleasure of letting a child play with others of their age and inclination. I chose to accept that as the reason, and reflected that that people just plain enjoyed the simple, no-frills joys of living in this spectacular environment. This was as close to finding the "television version" of Montana that we ever found.

My close ties to the parks people offered us unique moments which stay with me today: learning about a "TV tuning chair" straddling an old cabin's roof used by the cabin's occupants to climb up and then manually fine tune the reception, every night. We watched, in soft contentment, a herd of more than a hundred bison calmly cross the U-shaped valley of the Lamar River at dusk. We spied grizzlies at a safe distance across a meadow while hiking. We drove a buckboard wagon across the high plains to a field camp. We shared an early April "snow tunnel" of a road with a herd of bison, each bigger than our SUV. Like getting to know a few of the people who lived there, these were all instants which I never would have experienced in such serendipitous, genuine, and uncontrived situations.

The Montana experience was hard to process in total. Balanced with this incredibly different experience for a city-born guy like myself, Montana was a damned hard place in which to do business. And it is indeed ironic that the "Empty Promises" campaign which saved my job and the Montana Power Company account was called that. For it is a sad historical fact that "Empty Promises" has sort of been the theme of the American West expansion for over 200 years. People came to Montana and a lot of other places across the West on promises that were empty and unrealized. Native Americans too, were repeatedly given such empty promises. Line your pockets with gold. Cattlemen, farmers, miners... the list goes on for hundreds of years.

In Montana, some clients were gracious and polite. Others would just as soon cut your fiscal throat as they would look you in the eye and call you a friend. It was often an indifferent and even a cruel place, especially for an outlander like me; resented from the get-go and made to feel like the root cause of all evil xenophobic things under the sun.

We really did not belong here. Try as we might, this kept coming back at us, stronger at every turn. The need to leave was obvious to my wife early on; but being a too-stubborn fellow, I hung on way too long. It got to me slowly and by the time I realized we had to leave we had spent ten long years trying to make it all work. We had learned a lot about the ins and outs of Montana. It was time to go. Somewhere, not here.

So, I left my partner Ryan, left our small and struggling ad agency, and it nearly broke my heart. He was so deeply talented, and the two of us could have gone anywhere. But he would not leave; his family and his wife's family were there. He had his music, and also had made a name for himself doing fine art. Many friends. He had a lot going on. This was his hometown, but not mine. I left in order to give my family something more than that place ever could. And I told him that. But of course, it wasn't leaving Montana that broke me in two, it was the act of leaving him behind. More than 20 years later, I still wish it had been somehow different.

A POET'S LEGACY ON A RAZOR'S EDGE

CHAPTER VI: ALL THE BEAUTIFUL PEOPLE COULD KILL YOU

We moved to Washington State at the urging of a good friend, and I joined up with another ad agency. Daniel is a long-distance runner and got into this sport in Bend Oregon, ground zero for distance running in the United States and beyond. Distance running is a sport that is quite self-selective. It requires a very high degree of dedication, the willingness to put up with sacrifice, pain and determination. It was a great proving ground for Daniel. And after that he would remark that almost found the profession of copy writing easy in comparison.

You know how English people swallow their consonants at times? I remember a Monte Python skit in which a fellow is described as "So English he can hardly speak." Monte Python was always rich in its ability to tease in a good-natured manner. In a similar sense I (will always) believe that Daniel is so multi-dimensionally intelligent that he can hardly talk. He sometimes has a hard time completing sentences and I have always thought it was because his brain is going so fast and in so many directions at once, that he can hardly get across a thought before 10 other equally interesting thoughts are crowding the entrance door that is his mouth. And then he wondrously diverges without indication or explanation, and he is off on another subject. The effect is sometimes a jazz-like agglomeration of different things, as one were "conversing" via piano with Herbie Hancock or Dave Brubeck. I love talking with him. It is always inspiring.

Daniel helped me land a job with this incredibly creative agency. And when I was shown my new office right next to the creative department, I fell in love with the boisterous energy of the place. Best of all, my new office was painted in psychedelic hues of blue and purple, felt like it was a wing of the stage at SNL, had an almost antique desk, tall ceilings and – a nice old-world couch! Not leather, but hey, a damn couch! Hey, I had not had a couch in many years, so this seemed a bonus!

But the politics and tension at this agency! Oh brother! Back when I was in Montana there were politics aplenty, hurt egos everywhere, often because there were people there who had no business trying to be in advertising. And through my earlier mentioned maneuvers with Montana Power, I got a master class in tiptoeing through that minefield.

But that was the bushiest of bush leagues insofar as politics went.

This agency I joined in Spokane Washington was of a different class entirely. Unlike the agency in Montana, there was genuine talent at this place. We often had outrageously good creative – we were known for it. (My friend Daniel was the driving force behind much of it when I joined.) But oh, the screaming... we had people in the creative group who routinely threw temper tantrums that included the ripping up of concepts, histrionic fits, slamming doors, silent treatments and behavior that even a middle-school kid would find embarrassing. I never saw any physicality, but it would not have surprised me.

My couch became known as the "crying couch." When people had reached their limit (as happened with distressingly great regularity in this crazy place) they would come into my office and... they'd cry. I absolutely hated that. I never knew what to do or say when people just lose it like that. Men *and* women. But for some reason, this was the place in which to lose it. (Maybe it had been that place historically and I was just the most recent "owner" of the crying couch.) I had a *lot* of tearful visitors. I took to having tissues on hand. And candies. I felt awkward, often.

What made this even worse: the senior shareholders mostly tolerated this hyper-emotional sort of environment as the price of doing business. While a few of the 'bad boys' were verbally reprimanded, to my knowledge nobody was ever fired for this sort of immature conduct. This affected morale and, like selective enforcement does, had a toxic and cumulative effect on many of the less crazy people there. In the end this was the seed of the agency's unraveling. But I am getting ahead of myself.

ALL OUR TOMORROWS END TODAY

Sometime during a four-day Christmas party trip to see various clients in Oregon and Washington, I fell ill. I felt run down, and after the trip I decided to stay home in bed to recover. Except, I did not recover.

My skin felt weird; my right leg felt weird. Very achy, oddly numb and strangely puffy, except the puffiness felt like soft serve ice cream; or crackly ice cream... it would move around under my fingers and then just sit there without bouncing back. I lay there in bed, thinking, "This does not seem good at all."

The next morning, I found to my surprise that I could hardly sit up. I got dressed in some work out sweats. My wife had to help me out to the car, and then she drove me to the Urgent Care center. At first, they did some procedures. Then, suddenly and with worrying urgency, they rushed me into an operating room and hurriedly put me under. I was quite panicked at the sudden, rapid speed of their actions. When I awoke, I was in tremendous pain and apparently tried to punch someone. They explained that it looked like "a bomb had gone off" under my skin. All through my abdominal wall and down my right leg, the layer under my skin had liquified. At this point they did not know precisely why this happened, or how to treat it. I learned about a week later that I had somehow contracted a very rare bacterial infection that usually required debridement (like what you would do for a burn patient) or amputation of the infected areas in order to save my life.

I thought I might not make it out of there. I spent about the next 10 days in the ICU, perhaps more. The ICU is a very disturbing place in which to spend any time as a patient. While nobody told me about my prognosis, I easily sensed that ICUs are a place of bad company. Everyone around me was dying. Therefore...

I did not want to finish that thought. But I did, privately, and often.

It was an odd mix of feelings, lying in that ICU, figuring the probabilities of survival. It was not quite fear, but it had some panic. Mostly my emotions at the time were a mixture of anger and sadness. I was angry and sad that this might be all I get after the whole amazing life I had been able to live so far. After all the wonderful things I had seen, shared with my wife, and all the incredible challenges I had faced... That this dumb and sterile place is where I might die; lying here in some stinky, bloody bandages. What a shitty way for this to end. I was disappointed.

The experience itself was a bit like what I always thought a corpse-strewn battlefield would feel like if you were wounded, abandoned and could not get up. It was like a series of black-out sketches, scored with opera music: a wide assortment of sights and sounds.

Snippets of other peoples' sufferings: I heard sons and daughters, crying and weeping over loved ones. I would fall asleep. When I awoke, the objects of the sadness, desperation, love... they were suddenly gone. This room was about the last moments. I heard last rites being delivered to people. Sounds of sobbing. Bits of whimpers. The rolling of beds, in and out. In and out. And by morning, all of the people lying near me... gone.

Through these and other moments of consciousness, I sensed that people were dying all around me. Over and over and over. I so very desperately, with all my soul, did not want to be in this terrible place.

There was good news and bad news. The good news is that the doctors had figured out what was wrong: I had somehow gotten infected with flesh-eating bacteria. The bad news, aside from that horribly-sounding diagnosis, was that the survival rate was only about 5%. And worse, it usually involved amputation. And worse, some of this infection was in my abdomen.

It was worrisome.

Lying in this ICU, I sensed that there were two exits... And that most people went through that one, dreaded eternal door. I thought that this was it. Really it. The end. I concluded that my time was up. The odds were that I was going to die. Soon. My heart was full of regret... regret that I'd be leaving everyone and everything I so dearly and desperately loved. I did not want to go.

But then one night, I felt something that I can only describe as gigantic in the truest sense of the word. Overwhelming. A force or a sense of something. Maybe it was my brain being washed in survival chemicals. Maybe it was God. Maybe it was nothing at all. But – and here is the thing – in its aftermath (the perceived presence of which I am not able to ever begin to express) I was absolutely convinced that everything would be okay. That I would be okay. That I would not die. I somehow knew this deeply and with absolute certainty.

The reader will recall that I had not been a religious person. I really did not know if I believed in a god, or a creator. Or anything. But this moment, like some others I have experienced in life, was totally beyond explanation. The surety of my optimism was total. And this feeling, real or not, caused by internal or external forces... it matters not. What matters is that this gave me respite. This gave me shelter. It allowed me to deal with this horrible, painful reality with a courage and conviction that had not been possible, and which I had not known before.

Time was hard to grasp. I came in and out of consciousness. I knew that my body was in extreme pain. But now it felt manageable. Because I knew it would be okay. It would wash over and beyond me, impersonally. As odd and uncomfortable as it sounds, pain became something that I learned to know intimately and almost clinically. It had colors, flavors, tones and shades, and was something that became a state of existence. Like turning the light on, or off.

We moved into treatment phase. They had figured out, they thought, how to actively stop the infection, reverse it and save my life. I perceived dimly that there were now many doctors on the team overseeing my situation. My primary doctor, a young fellow, was (like me) a long-distance bicyclist. There was repeated discussion of possibly having to amputate my right leg, about mid-thigh in order to save my life. There was discussion of antibiotic treatment on my abdomen – the other infected region which could not be amputated – but which might work. People would have these sorts of discussions at my bedside, thinking I was not there. But I *was* there. Listening and mostly understanding. I did not let on, lest they have discussions away from me. But I understood the key concepts, and kept it to myself.

I felt like a prisoner.

I had fifteen surgeries in about 18 days, each to clean my wounds in a sterile operating room, and to go to extreme measures to save my abdomen. Honestly it was one of the most repeatedly frightening things I have experienced. Each time I did not know the condition in which I would wake up, or if I would wake up at all.

They fed me with intense antibiotics and painkillers for weeks. After several weeks, my infection had slowed but had not reversed. I was tested every two days to monitor progress. More and more areas were showing signs of spreading infection. I was still sinking.

But... wait. I had been told by whatever visited me that night, that I would be okay. So why was the infection continuing? This is not what was supposed to happen. I was supposed to have turned the corner. But the testing said otherwise: it showed that I was getting worse.

My family in Chicago wanted to fly in to see me. I knew it was because everyone anticipated that this was the death watch. I knew it. I told them "No." I was not ready for this final bedside scene.

My wife, a Registered Nurse, was very good at keeping me up to date on everything. She was upbeat but honest: I knew it was not looking good. I was in horrible shape: I had lost about 30% of my body weight. I was gray in skin tone. I could tell I was circling the drain. But in this moment, my brother did something I will never forget: he bravely came despite my request to stay home. He came. When later asked if I enjoyed his visit, I had no memory of it. But he came. Even in our (then) on-and-off-again relationship, he tossed it all aside, and showed up for me.

My wife had been putting in many nights of deep medical research on this rare infection. And in her web-based research she read about Hyperbaric Chambers. They were a relatively advanced and unexplored bit of technology at the time: they simulated deep-sea pressures and in doing so forced oxygen into deep tissues. She found out that a hospital right down the road had in the past several weeks installed such a chamber in support of a Navy Submarine Warfare unit that was stationed almost inexplicably nearby. This infection hated oxygen and if this worked, the oxygen would help to kill the infection and open up the possibility of letting me recover. We might get in there, she suggested to our doctor.

Our lead doctor shut her down, saying that there was no science behind it, just some anecdotal evidence. Not enough to warrant such a two-hospital collaboration, he said. But Ann persisted and petitioned the total team who watched over me to reconsider. She won.

They signed the order for the hyperbaric chamber procedures, and we figured out an insurance-approved, 2x per day transportation to and from this other hospital for two one-hour sessions, one in the morning and then again in the afternoon, for two weeks.

I was their second patient, ever.

At this point I had been hospitalized for almost three weeks, and my lower muscles had become jelly. I was, not too long ago, a guy who happily rode 50 miles at a time on my bicycle. Now, I could not even sit up, let alone walk. I remember the incredibly difficult transfer from bed, to gurney, to ambulance, to hyperbaric chamber slide, to gurney, to bed. Twice a day. I would have to rest twice or three times per transfer. It was like sprint-riding uphill... totally and completely exhausting; I had no strength at all.

The hyperbaric chamber itself was incredibly small, the plexiglass was less than an inch or two from any part of my now rail-thin body. They gave me a plastic bladder of water and a straw to sip from during my sessions. Each session lasted about 30 minutes. It was claustrophobically panic-inducing, but I got used to it.

Gradually, after several days of this, my grueling bed, then gurney, then chamber transfers seemed like they were getting slightly easier to endure. At first, I questioned my own perceptions, suspecting this was just wishful thinking. But I definitely felt like my overall body pain was lessening, and my mental concentration increased. I felt my strength begin to return. My color improved. I began taking on weight. I was getting better; I could feel it.

Knowing that I was a guy who liked goals and processes, Ann put together a "work" schedule for me for each day, and placed it on the wall of my hospital room. So insightful, my wonderful wife. She knew that I liked purpose. And not only did I have a purpose, I had a goddamned plan, things to do. And I applied myself to it like any other schedule. This was my job. This was *The Job*: the only job that counted.

The fellows at the agency: they came and visited. They assured me that I was missed, and that my job would be held open for my return. This gave me hope. This cemented a bond. This was a spirit-lifting thing that they did not have to do, but did. It out-shouted every other weird and immature thing about that odd climate, and defined my personal loyalty to them, from then on.

The people at the Hyperbaric Chamber – you could see it on their faces – they were happy and fulfilled, and helping to save my life. It was a glorious thing. After the first two weeks, satisfied with the success that I was having, the team managing the hyperbaric chamber got me on another rotation. I continued to excel. My every-other-day diagnostic tests showed that the infection had stopped. And now it was actually *receding*. And then one day, after my prognosis diagnostic tests, it was simply gone. There were no "lights," no markers. There was zero infection. Gone.

Was it really gone? I hoped so, but did not know for sure. I did not let my guard down for an instant. Like those bad vampire movies, I kept an eye over my shoulder just waiting for it to strike back. Happily, it never came back.

After all this crazy crap, I survived.

And here I was again. Another razor's edge. Like so many moments, where things could have gone either way, so easily. Just like that day back in the 1970s in my parent's living room: yet another brand-new possible timeline was being rewritten, starting right now, at this moment.

Just weeks before, I had been staring into a deep dark hole in the Universe, and here I was: with the sudden realization that yet again, I get to Live. I could not believe that I was still here.

And the root cause here: plainly, it was the woman I married. I remain convinced that if not for her persistence this nasty infection would have killed me just like it killed 95% of the others who got it. Period. I had always said that marrying her was the best thing I ever did. And, not like I ever needed any clarity on that point, but man, this made it crystal clear!

Now it was time for me to come back to a normal life, whatever type of "normal" I might be able to manage. Physically, I was a shambles: I was able to get up out of my bed but I had to relearn to walk, climb stairs, and relearn every other damn thing that involved my torso and leg muscles. I used a walker at first: doing laps around the hospital floor. Dripping in sweat, I attacked this as though I was training for the Olympics. This was The Job. And I was determined to come back. My mantra was "110%." Yes, I had a limp. Yes, I had a tremendous amount of pain. But it would pass, and I was coming back!

I left the hospital after about 45 days. I had a t-shirt that said "Sole Survivor" and pictured a mountain climber reaching the top of a precipice. I wore it on that fine day. I could walk short distances, slowly and with a pretty significant limp. I had to move gradually.

I could not climb stairs very well. Or get up out of a chair without assistance. I still had open wounds that took months to close fully and of their own accord. But I made it back. Within a year I could move just as well as ever, and then I got even stronger, determined to succeed.

I have found that there is a purity in struggle against an identifiable foe. Such pure moments, such perfectly elemental moments are usually the stuff of storybooks or legends; usually something we read about in sagas and tales from a distant time.

This is the weird part of my experience: In day-to-day life, it is rare to have a singular foe or a clear path to vanquishing that foe. But this is precisely what I had, at that moment in my life. I felt like I faced a terrifying dragon of staggeringly immense power and size. I had the dragon in my sights. Courtesy of something – God, the universe, brain chemicals – I had been given a shield: my conviction. I had been "told" that I would be okay. But, like in any battle, a simple shield just protects you for a bit.

But a shield alone is not enough to actually slay the dragon. For that, you need a weapon. Through her persistence, my wonderful wife had provided the weapon, right when I needed it most: the hyperbaric chamber. This is what I needed to slay that dragon. And together, we killed the bastard!

A reporter wanted to do a series on me. He and other people have asked if I saw a light, or felt God or something like that. I wish I could have said yes. But that would not be true. What I experienced – or more accurately felt—was the purity of elemental struggle for my own life.

The focus and elemental simplicity of that battle were unlike anything I have experienced. This terrible and painful event proved to be a life-affirming thing. This may not make sense to some people. It might even strike some people as strange. It was in the end an arduous but extremely valuable journey.

I emerged from the hospital and clawed slowly and deliberately back to the life I had enjoyed before. That first new spring is one I will always remember for the feeling of significant victory we enjoyed. I remember the buds of daffodils bursting through the snow. And the trees showing signs of new growth. We bought a sports car that spring. And a motor boat. I thanked whoever or whatever was listening (the Universe or God or something) for "this life," every day. For years thereafter.

I knew this was now my bonus round: the life I almost did not get. So, we lived every day like there was nothing on earth that could stop us. And that is exactly how we felt.

And what of the Early Demise Hypothesis? On the day I left that hospital wearing my "Sole Survivor" t-shirt, I decided that I had cheated death; I killed the Early Demise Hypothesis, right along with that other dragon, the infection. I killed it, forever.

BETWEEN AOL AND FACEBOOK

This bonus round of life: We lived in a small white house in a forest of tall pines. Deer and the occasional moose wandered by. We had trails for hiking and cross-country skiing within ten minutes. Apple orchards and rural character, and great big lakes. My wife had a good nursing job with nice people, our daughter was a sports star at her high school, and my job was on the ups. What a great gift we enjoyed in this new life!

The ad agency I joined was quite advanced: it had, all the way back in 1996, an interactive group. We were building high quality web sites back then. This, for grounding purposes, was when AOL was "cutting edge." It was a full decade before the iPhone. It was about the time that Apple nearly went out of business. It was when Nintendo had the Game Boy... And during these prehistorically backward technological times, our agency, by contrast, was webbier than anyone around. We had an interactive group with coders, and flash designers and HTML types. It was nothing short of amazing.

We worked with Nintendo and several other technology companies, doing attractive and useful business-based web sites, gaming web sites, banner ads, page takeovers and even interstitial ads. We handled the back-end internet databases for several national brands. We hosted sites on our own servers. We were extremely far ahead of the market in our ability to program and our advanced skills won us clients that we never might have even been able to talk to otherwise. We had national recognition, and won several of the first Webby awards ever awarded! For all our trail-blazing, we got a ton of work from Seattle-based clients and in time opened an office there to handle a large and growing part of the business.

But against this, agency life was tough and sometimes terribly harsh. I was in charge of client services (account people, planners, media) and had to routinely both hire and cut people from the roster. In my least favorite moment, I had to fire an account executive because the "client fit was not right." In this case, the essence of the client fit was that the mean girls on the client side felt that my account exec was not the type of person they wanted to hang out with. "I mean, just look at her shoes," one muttered as proof of the issue. It was not the work that was at fault, it was her personality, somehow manifested most egregiously in her choice of shoes. This sucked.

The dominant guy at the agency came from the media side of the world. Jimmy was a car guy and made custom hot rods. He was a fast and big talker. By personality he was aggressive, prone to misogyny and had classic narcissistic tendencies. Trumpy well before the age of Trump. His partner, who owned a little less than he did but still about half the agency, balanced this out through his Jesuit-scholar style and his very empathetic and measured approach. Honestly, without this second partner, I might not have lasted a year with them.

Their third, and very junior partner, who owned a nominal number of shares, grew up on the wrong side of the tracks. Hey that happens. I did in a way, too. Thing is, this will define you, but only if you let it. He did. His rough roots dug at him incessantly. So, he overcompensated: he had all the status symbols acquired and on display, at all times, in order to assemble a facade of taste and sophistication. It was not enough to have a glamorous designer watch. He had to make sure you knew about it, and how much he paid for it. He was needy but in this odd and sometimes sad way.

In short, he was a perpetually insecure guy who constantly needed affirmation in order to keep his insecurities from taking over. As a result, dealing with him was exhausting. And at times, dangerous. We'll call him Lerdo.

Lerdo liked social climbing and basketball and his wave runners. His job was to act as chief lackey for our biggest account, the Major Wireless Company. The fact that they kicked him repeatedly like a dog only added to his all-consuming insecurity.

I found out all of these things about Lerdo about eight months into working there. For all his issues, he was sort of unstable when you got to know him a bit. It was a little frightening, because Lerdo was that sort of person who would throw monkey wrenches into the mix just to cause chaos. And with this sneaky sabotage, he would try to take everyone down as many pegs as possible.

Despite these issues, I suppose I could have left for something else. But at this point in life, having this job allowed us to live in this outdoor recreational paradise where we could boat, ski, or hike just about every day in epic places, within a few miles of our cozy house in the woods. All things have to find balance, and this was our balance for a long and lovely time.

GOLDEN ARCHES

We were always on the hunt for new business, and I became the "go to" guy when it suited the owners of the business (in other words when they did not want to do it).

Given that we were the biggest ad agency in this neck of the woods, we caught the attention of a group that managed McDonalds in parts of Washington, Oregon and Idaho. They reached out to us about possibly competing in a pitch for their advertising business. There were about 30 owner operators involved, covering over a hundred stores in both urban and rural areas.

We were one of three ad agencies asked to participate in the review. The other two agencies involved included an international firm that had the inside track: they already handled the international corporate account for McDonalds, and knew fast food inside and out. The third firm was also interesting: a super-regional firm from LA that specialized in this category and handled the advertising for many such regions for McDonalds across the Western US. And here we were, the number three choice. David versus two Goliaths. It was a bit troubling.

We had *zero* experience in the restaurant business. We had *zero* credentials in Fast Food. We even had *zero* experience working with advertising associations. In total then, objectively we had zero business even pitching this account.

So, that meant that I was the leader of the "lost cause" team. The long shot special. Out-manned, out-gunned, and out-classed. Frankly, the owners gave this hot potato to me because they figured there was no chance in hell that we'd win, and they did not want to be the losers.

This was like a moon shot. But all we really had was a bottle rocket. If we won, this would be significant both in profit and revenue. If we won, this would become the second biggest client in the shop aside from a big mobile phone company out of Seattle. It would also be a highly strategic win: increasing our share of media versus other agencies in this part of the country. The added media clout would be like a market-size play: giving us better deals, more attention and increased weight across all our media partners, and benefitting all our clients' media budgets.

The pitch was being coordinated through McDonald's regional offices in Seattle. The briefing document laid out the requirements of the successful firm: marketing skills, media management skills, the ability to manage the association (meetings, agenda, walking through procedures, etc.) and interfacing with corporate to measure results and perform budget oversight. It was, as RFQs go, an extensive and very detailed document.

Having personally done a tiny bit of association management in the past (for car dealers—a very tough group), and having done many situation analyses when I was with Landor, I knew that personal connections were everything. So, I asked if the people in charge of the review process if we would be allowed to visit all 30 owner operators to understand their issues, face-to-face. Corporate reminded us that this was a logistical nightmare, with the stores and owner-operators being widely scattered across three states. They questioned whether we were really willing to do this. But I reiterated that yes, indeed we were ready to do this. They approved it, and we were off!

It was indeed a major investment in time, fuel and patience. I personally did all of the interviews, and brought with me either our media director or the account person that I'd have working with me on the business. We visited all 30 owner operators in about two weeks' time. Each one-on-one session lasted, depending on interest and availability, from 30 minutes to over 2 hours.

McDonalds owner-operators are, as one might suspect, both a strong and opinionated lot. And rightfully so; the operation of a series of stores (each owner operator usually had between 2 and 5 stores) is a complex, frustrating managerial nightmare. It pays well, but it's as tough and 24/7 a type of gig as one could ever take on.

We listened closely to each owner operator's needs, issues, etc. Our most valuable question was "What qualities will the successful agency have in spades?"

Armed with all 30 responses and mountains of notes, we set up a war room back at the agency, then coalesced and managed their extensive feedback. We used their precise issues as a framework for both our presentation and written response piece. While the presentation "rules" specified the things we needed to cover, we basically threw that out. We nodded to them in principle, winked and did our own thing. We talked to them only about the things they found important.

In business pitches, I have a few firm beliefs which I have used to very positive effect through the years.

Most importantly, I believe that people hire people first, then firms second. This has significant implications for how one conducts a winning pitch:

First, while I understand the role of business development people in moving along an opportunity, I believe it is vital to keep the group to the smallest possible team who actually will be working, day-by-day, on the business. The Cast of Thousands approach hardly ever wins the day. I believed it then and I believe it now.

Second, assembling pitches is much like developing an ad: be persuasive, but keep it focused, keep it relevant and make it fun.

Third, I have been in pitches that were horrible in their size and scope: hopelessly over-staffed, over-scripted, devoid of personality and too crowded with people, points of view, benefits and confusing to the prospective clients. It is analogous to ads which have too many copy points and in the end, do nothing well.

Fourth, in setting the parameters and roles, it is best to give each of the participants time to be people, and not give them so much content and or coaching to paint them into the corner and make them mere presentation robots. This means giving them 'air' and letting them riff a bit. This allows people to get to know them as people, not cardboard functionary puppets from Company XYZ.

Fifth, I coach my people to act as a team. Throw the ball around. Have fun with each other. That shows each person's humanity and lets the audience get closer to knowing us as people. Because in the end we are people, and we hire people just as much as we hire companies.

Finally, as in developing an ad, you need to be relevant. You need to talk way more about them. Only talk about you as a way to offer quality assurance. Same with your client roster: only mention it as a quality assurance item, as in, hire us and you 'belong to this club.'

With these guidelines in mind, you can almost imagine our presentation. The three of us who did the interviews, also did the *entire* pitch. This gave each of us a lot of face time, and in the interview sessions we equally used that time to create one-to-one relationships with each of the owner operators. When we came in then, they knew us already. We'd spent time together. Had a Coke together. Maybe a burger. The ice was already broken.

In most business pitches, the lead person often performs 'master of ceremonies' duties with little actual heavy lifting in the presentation. I absolutely hate that. No ceremonial heads in my boat. No free rides on my team. I have always believed in leading from the front. So here, as in every presentation I have led, I took a deep and active role. Heavy lifting. What did I do? I talked about *them*. Their issues, their needs, the priorities they had all voiced. How we would help them in each and every way. Concrete things, no hand waving or magic. *Substance*. I had the visibility that they did not: I had actual data on how many of them felt differently about topics a, b, c, et cetera. And I used that to make them pay attention to what we were about to say.

Them, them, them. Our media director talked about local media and the things we could do for them. Our account exec talked about marketing research we had done on what people thought of McDs and its core competitors. Again, we each talked about them, not us. Each of us talked about them. We had good content, room to breathe, and highly relevant things to say. We tossed the ball around. We had as much fun as our nerves allowed. We followed that up with a longer-than-normal Q&A session. We had prepped two owner operators with a few possible Qs, to get the ball rolling. And it rolled very well.

Other agencies had twice and three times the number of people. And the commonly asked question at the end of the pitch was, "Will all of you be actively involved on this account on a daily basis?" And of course, they had to dance around that. But at a certain level people usually know when the BS comes down. And the one agency with nine people got caught flatfooted. Clients typically hate that bait-and-switch, and the super-regional agency who specialized in fast food and in McDonald's owner-operator groups? Well, they got shut down right here, on their paltry answer to this very question, right on this very presentation stage.

In the end it was between us and the huge international incumbent agency. The client pushed us on our pricing, thinking that this was such a large media account that we would operate at a loss in other (creative and account) areas. Doubly so, they figured they could use the incumbent agency as leverage. They were wrong. Over three subsequent meetings on budget with the officers of the association we held tough. And in the end, we prevailed! We won this account fair and square. And we priced things so it made sense for both parties.

Working on this account proved to be much more complex and intellectually rewarding than any of us could have imagined. First, their point-of-sale systems were so good that it was possible for us to know how many items of every possible configuration had been sold the very next day, in each store and market. The value of that immediacy was huge, allowing us to change out messaging in electronic media in order to manage demand and traffic. Not enough sales of Sausage McMuffin and Egg (SMEs)? Swap out our lunch messaging for that instead. Stores running out of Ice Cream Parfaits? Kill that ad and run messages on full breakfast deals. Endless possibilities.

The second and unannounced wrinkle in working with McDs was that the agencies were actually in charge of proposing the calendar of marketing tactics. This meant 1) determining the promotions, 2) assembling the economics of the promotion (cost of goods, sales price, gross profit) and then proposing the manner in which this will be supported (mass media, in store displays, contests, promotions, etc.). In short, we acted not only as the ad agency, but also as the association's marketing team!

We had never done any of this before, so we learned quickly. While this was certainly a way to stretch our skills, it also provided us an interesting and unforeseen opportunity which, as it turned out, allowed us to make a significant impact on McDonalds in the US.

The first year of working with McDonalds was a learning experience. Much of the learning involved the finer points of the tricky interpersonal politics of the owner-operator board, and how the overlay of the complex relationship that Corporate had with the Owner-Operators. This group had a large number of very strong, opinionated and often rational people. But at the same time, a significant number of the owner-operators worked from a less metrics-based and more intuitively-based place. One such person was the fellow rumored to have started the value meal concept at McDonalds. As such, he had a lot of political clout within the organization and among owner-operators across the US. Also on our board were a few guys who were really good with financials and who were incredibly persuasive. The finesse of helping these guys get the marketing calendars they needed was all in making sure their considerable strengths were leveraged when we got marketing calendars 'sold in' at the corporate level. Corporate, through their levers of quality control, financing and real estate, could make it tough on owner operators with whom they had issues.

Along the way in working up our marketing program calendar for year #2, our team got smarter about working the McDonalds' system – we found out that we could research marketing tactics used by other associations across the US. We could see what each and every association did: what worked, and what did not. This was a great database which we could treat as a series of test cases for various marketing tactics. After much digging, we found one group of stores in upstate New York that had done a promotion which resulted in almost immediate, significant and – for the life of the promotion –

lasting and recurring sales increase. They had put together a menu of things you could get for a dollar. To support this they did signage, outdoor, radio promotion and menu placards.

With this evidence and some testimonials from the association in upstate New York in hand, we dove deeper. We ran our own numbers. We had access to the cost of goods sold for every menu item. And we had an estimate of the operational complexity (manhours) for any item. With this and a rapidly growing excel spreadsheet, we added to this and war-gamed out a few different scenarios on the costs for media and in-store support, did our financial analysis and identified ten different menu items and bundles of items that would constitute a solid Dollar Deals menu. These items had variety, would be profitable at the store level, could be promoted as a grouping and done in a cost-effective manner... It looked like from a financial standpoint, this would work! We called it the Dollar Deals Menu.

We determined that if we got even half the uptick in sales of what had occurred in upstate New York we would generate acceptable returns, and if it generated best-case boosts in total sales volume and operator gross profit (rather than cannibalizing from other items), we'd keep it for the rest of the calendar year with a maintenance media schedule to periodically boost its top-of-mind recall.

It seemed clear (even though the financials were complex) and we proposed it to the core management team at our association. They loved it. Then we went further – we proposed that if it kept up, we would institutionalize it. The owner-operators liked that too.

We brought our new baby to the corporate team, quite excited about what we were about to do. To our surprise, the corporate office fought our recommendation quite hard. They cited the fact that food prices would gradually creep up (which is true) and this was going to be eventually unsustainable (also true), but I felt there was something else at the core of this resistance... I wondered what on earth could be wrong with this picture.

Then I thought about how corporate makes their money, which is quite different from how franchisees make theirs. While I could not prove it, I suspected that corporate may have feared other and deeper business outcomes: namely that 1) this would work, 2) other associations would also adopt it, 3) this widespread change would alter the corporation's total beef volume (smaller burgers were featured on the Dollar Menu and would sell at higher volumes than bigger burgers) and further, it was conceivable that such a shift in the size of burgers would lessen the total tonnage of beef that McDonalds was buying from its South American producers.

Considering the size of such major contracts with big beef producers, this shift might, in turn, have the effect of making beef more expensive per pound for the corporation. This rise in beef prices would ultimately put the corporation in a profit squeeze situation when they sold it to the franchisees.

This was, of course, all supposition on my part. But it makes sense to follow the money and simply think like an accountant to understand some corporations' actions.

In the end, we won the day and got our Dollar Deals Menu launched. We did it by leveraging the will of our owner-operator group and the political clout that some of these people had within the larger franchisee organization.

I will admit that this was pretty scary for us: our immediate corporate contacts were quite antagonistic and threatening to us. They implied that if this did not work, our agency contract would be put into question.

Despite corporate's very hard-fought obstacles our owner operators embraced the plan. We launched the initiative, and to our delight it was immediately embraced by consumers. Our owner-operators saw huge gains in total sales and gross profits. While there was a little cannibalization in the first few months of other bigger ticket items, the same store profit increases more than made up for it, and in time, even the sales of larger sandwiches climbed back. We were growing both topline and bottom line after about 6 months of sales.

The program continued per our arrangement with our store owners, and in time Dollar Deals was adopted across the US with corporate's blessing. You cannot argue with success.

From an advertising and marketing standpoint I think the lesson here is that you have to keep your eyes open and borrow ideas if you see them working. Finally, if you do all your calculations right, you need to stick to your projections and convictions. People who have different agendas of more immediate self-interest will say just about anything to stop you.

ENDINGS/BEGINNINGS

Remember Lerdo the Perpetually Insecure? The account guy on Major Wireless, Incorporated?

Here's the backstory: Way back when I started at this ad agency, Lerdo was falling out of favor. He sensed it. The two key partners asked me to meet with them "first thing in the morning," as they had something important to talk about. I knew why.

That evening as I was packing up to leave, Lerdo came into my office and, feeling the nearness of the blade to his throat, sat on my couch and wept. (Yes, this was the same crying couch where many had sat before.)

Now, Lerdo and I were not at all close. In fact, I pretty much disliked him from day one. But here he was, sitting on my couch weeping, sobbing. Big snotty sobbing. Almost a stranger to me at the time. Talk about awkward.

This was quite out of character for this fellow, with his string of new luxury cars, and who normally tried to be all bluster and swagger. I once went into Lerdo's office. Only once. He gestured me to sit in his guest chair. It was unnaturally shortened so that my butt was maybe 4 inches off the floor. His chair was behind a normally-scaled desk. My nose was about at desktop level. On one side of his desk was a menacing cartoon figurine pointing a ray gun... right at my head. This was how Lerdo treated his office guests.

Back to the crying couch: Between deep sobs, Lerdo told me that he feared for his job. He went on whimpering that if he did not have this job, his girlfriend would leave him, and he would have nothing. Nothing. (As I counted his cars, jet skis and other adult toys, one can readily imagine my internal reaction to his histrionic display.)

Even so, I felt bad for the guy. I did have empathy, even for people I did not like. So, on the following day, when the partners asked if we should cut him, I told the partners 'No, keep him.' And they did: they kept him on, firing two other associates instead.

Fast forward then to several years later, after we had McDonalds, and close to the end of my time with them. Across these intervening years, Lerdo had done a decent job keeping Major Wireless Company happy and profitable most of the time. Principally, as far as I could tell, his account skills involved keeping the clients' coffee warm, their cocktails flowing and getting them assorted off-book "perks." Such is the unsavory underbelly of agency life among some larger clients who were into payola and tchotchkes of various types.

At this time, the two major partners were getting close to retirement. Originally, they had planned to do a wider employee stock ownership, but when reality hit, they balked at the complexity and the length of time this would take. They wanted out, soon. Feeling some loyalty to Lerdo, they negotiated a leveraged buy-out with him alone. This left me and several others without a stake in the place we felt that we had built.

As soon as they turned the place over to him, he did what most insecure kings do with their next-in-line guy. He got rid of me, with surgical precision and in record time. During the holidays. It was cruel, spiteful and not at all surprising to me.

But as I said earlier, Karma has its way.

In the end, Lerdo was not able to run the agency. While he managed to keep the Major Wireless account afloat largely through his well-honed servile tactics, illicit favors and other undocumented items, this approach did not translate at all to other clients who could have cared less about these sorts of things. All they wanted was good advertising at a fair price. Thing is about Lerdo, other than being obsequious, he had terrible client skills. He did not even understand actual advertising (media, positioning, marketing, etc.). And then as for business skills... well, I felt that he had no business skills. So, his failure seemed like a natural consequence.

He was not at all able to win any significant new business. He lost most key clients (including McDonalds). He did not even understand basic finance. Notably, this series of bad outcomes triggered a bad-performance clause in the buy-out contract with the original partners. Seeing their agency rapidly being run into the ground, they took back control of the agency. But despite their efforts, it was too late and they never recovered. In time the last entrails of the agency were sold off to another firm, which was subsequently sold to a third firm. And so it goes

While Lerdo did get to marry his girlfriend, it proved to be a short-lived arrangement. In the end, records show that she ended up divorcing him during this period and dragged him through the courts for almost eight years, taking most of his money and the house in the process.

Karma wins again.

So, to review: While we were in lovely and agrarian Spokane, I was out of a job, courtesy of Lerdo the Insecure. And he was in the process of skuttling the ad agency.

Oh well. Jobs (and kingdoms) come and go. It is important that when the ship begins to sink, while you can jump ship or not, it is most important to make sure you are not tied to the mast.

The only reason I had not jumped ship before the order came to walk the plank is that alternate ships in these parts were few and far between. While I was not too concerned about the future, I also did not see any light on the horizon.

I suppose it is like how a sailor in a life raft must feel: Day after day of poor results. Salt water from horizon to horizon, wind and waves. Yet you continue on, as you have no choice, with an eye toward the weather, knowing that that time just keeps ticking away. It's that ever-present tick-tick-tick that gnaws at you.

I loved living in Spokane for its slower pace of life, wonderful recreational opportunities and a surprisingly good live music scene. We were quite happy here in our little house in the woods. I really did not want to leave, but after about six months of uninspiring openings, dead-end leads and sometimes terrible coaching ("Maybe you might try doing web design?") I had to look more broadly at the rest of the world. I had to face the reality that better hunting grounds were out there. Lucky for me, I knew something about the big world beyond.

I got busy: I developed some killer pitch books and sent them out to a number of people in markets up and down the coast, from Seattle to San Diego. The books looked like the sort of things that major market agencies might send a platinum prospect. I sent them to hiring managers and senior people at big agencies. I scoured the employment ads. I found two promising positions, both back in California.

One promising gig was with a major international ad agency in their LA office, on a car company account! The hiring manager asked if I got down to LA at all and I casually said that I get there 'quite regularly.' (I lied.) Could I be there to meet him for dinner next week? Well, of course I could. I hustled. With an eye on my dwindling bank balance, I booked flights and a room and a car and went down to LA to explore this possibility.

All the car rental company had at the time was a shitty panel van with some missing accent strips along one side. I took it. As I pulled into the swanky hotel parking lot amidst the Maserati's and Lambos in my damaged panel van, I just prayed that my interviewer was nowhere nearby. At least the muffler worked, I thought.

My anxiety subsided when I met this guy. All was quite pleasant. This English fellow was a literary sort who loved James Joyce and said I reminded him of Joyce both in looks and world view. (I figured that was positive.) He was an extremely interesting person, and had worked at a NYC firm called Interbrand (a Landor competitor). This LA position would report to him, and would lead the planning team at this agency's West Coast office, principally on this car account. We had lots in common, and enjoyed a long lingering dinner full of really great conversation. We hit it off extremely well; so much so that I was certain an offer would be forthcoming from him, and them.

I stayed in a nearby (much less swanky) hotel overnight. The next morning, I hit rush hour traffic on the 405 – the most central freeway in LA—and on the way back to the airport, sat in almost standstill traffic for nearly an hour, missing my flight out of LAX. I eventually made it home, but not without reflecting on the reality that is Los Angeles.

About this time this lead came in, I also developed one with Ipsos-ASI, a global leader in the field of ad research.

After my roller coaster of a life working with design firms and ad agencies over the better part of two decades, the thought of going back into the insights business was more than a little interesting.

And the possibility of joining a big firm with global clients would have offered a welcome change. So, while "going back" to a place has always had its dangers for disappointment, I also knew that San Francisco had always been my favorite place, warts and all.

At their request, I flew to SF. I met for almost two full days (!) with the President of Ipsos-ASI as well as the hiring manager for this open position. I liked the President very much and found him mighty interesting as a person. And as for the hiring manager? I got on famously with her, almost from the moment we shook hands. We had an immediate connection, the sort that you never can quite put a finger on. She reminded me in personality of many of the trusted friends I'd had over the years, the kind you just shared the same wavelength with. Before the interviews concluded, she invited me to come to their bigger office in Chicago, where she worked, the following week. There, I was to meet with about eight other people and at the end of that gauntlet, do a presentation of research work I had done so they could see me "in action."

This next meeting in Chicago was quite thorough and exhausting. I met with about eight of the people who would be my peers. I liked each and every one of them: genuine, smart, empathetic to a person. Nearing the end of that long day of interviews, I was tasked with doing my hour-long presentation of some research I had done on creative we had developed to all of these VP+ level people. Saving this to the last was a test of both my endurance as well as my presentation skills.

Luckily, I loved presenting. It was second nature, and I considered it my stage. PowerPoint was my backup band and lead instrument all rolled into one. After all, at this point much of my job for the past 30 years had involved presentation, and having literally been working with PowerPoint intensely since the day after it launched, I quite likely had more PowerPoint experience than almost anyone on the planet. I was able to make PowerPoint do pretty much anything other than drive my car.

So, this was "best for last," major fun. I showed them interesting creative, thorough research, eye popping visuals, a few subtle animations and incorporated a select few well-calibrated PowerPoint tricks carefully, like a chef uses flavors. Sparingly. There were smiles all around. We ended with a very nice and interactive Q&A (my favorite part). I passed the whole day with flying colors.

I got really attractive offers from both firms. In the end, there was something really good about Ipsos-ASI. They seemed caring, cultural and had a bit of a conspiratorial flair. It fit me like nothing had before. The people were eclectic and creative. And interesting. And real. And frankly, the decision to go with Ipsos-ASI and return to San Francisco was the easiest career decision I ever made.

I realized that the interviewing process at Ipsos-ASI taught me that a deep, careful interview process is as important for the interviewee as it is the hiring manager. This gives everyone as thorough an understanding of the work, the people and the culture so that everyone gets to make an informed decision. And if it is a match, the partnership is solid for everyone concerned.

I ended up working for Ipsos longer than I worked for any other firm over my almost 45-year career.

CHAPTER VII: TO ARRIVE AT WHERE I STARTED

See, I am dancing!

On the rim of the world, I am dancing!"

Ohlone Tribal Song

I returned to San Francisco in the middle of the long July 4 weekend and settled into a temporary bachelor pad with uncomfortable rental furniture across the bay from the city itself. My wife had to stay behind for a bit to coordinate with the realtor, get us packed up, manage the selling of our house and to get our daughter off to college. She had her hands full. The summer dragged on but we all played our parts and pulled together as we needed to.

I commuted by ferry into SF each day; such a civilized option. Sometime during the first few weeks as we approached the city from the East, it was emerging through the fog and the entire waterfront shone with a golden light. I still have that (bad) cell phone photo somewhere, aside from the image in my mind's eye.

When I arrived the local Ipsos office housed two different client/ project teams but had no leader, and about three people (none of which were me) had been vying for that position. One was Jim, a self-centered but more or less harmless fellow who used too many acronyms and buzz words and tried too hard to 'act intelligent.' Net result: nobody could really understand him, but at the same time, nobody would openly admit that. And at first meeting, trying to track with him was sort of a back-and-forth, as I oscillated between "maybe I'm just an idiot" to "man, what is going on in that head of his."

Then there was Sue, a rail-thin, wound-too-tight person who was so rule-driven that she could not see the true road to pretty much anywhere. Finally, there was my predecessor Ellen, who had gone on maternity leave and who everyone said would be back at some point soon to take on "a major role" that nobody could or would explain. I wondered and worried about that last bit, as one might imagine.

My immediate team consisted of four people, the senior of whom was all the way in Cincinnati with another support person who reported to her. My two local support people were more or less a team, one junior, the other senior. Ryan, the senior person had "been promised" the position that had been given to me. No reasons were given for him not getting it, no history was shared. Just mystery. To make matters worse, whenever he and I talked he quickly shuffled things around and/or closed his computer. He looked all the world like he was either hiding something incriminating, or looking for something... also incriminating. It was a constant unsettling feeling with him. I secretly felt that Ryan might have been looking for a ghost gun with which to shoot me at any moment.

Shelley, my local junior-level person, was quite intelligent and helpful, but seemed to dangerously exude the over-confidence that junior people sometimes did. I should have noticed at the time: the troubling thing was that she did not have a *consistently* firm grasp on the many technicalities of our approach to ad testing. This proved dangerous.

So, Ryan was trying to sabotage me, and Shelley was not 100% reliable as an information source. These were the people in charge of teaching me the many intricacies of our metrics, norms and standards. Their error was then my error.

I inadvertently got compromised: while I did not trust Ryan, I believed in Shelley. And while many of the things Shelley said were correct, a few, as it turned out to our mutual surprise, were extremely incorrect. And it was a few of these things that tripped us up with a big client.

Lastly, there was Ellen, who I had replaced. She had gone on maternity leave in March, it was now July. They had been working without any real management oversight or quality control for several months. They currently reported on paper to a distant and overwhelmed SVP (who already had way too much on her plate to deal with). And Ellen, while a quite technically excellent researcher, had not done much along the lines of mentoring, supervising, teaching or coaching of her staff.

Moreover, there were no basic management tools in place: procedures, controls, check-ins. No reporting system. No pipeline for new business. Nothing. And for client relationships? All the client relationships had been one-to-one, with each of these people directly interfacing with clients and their organizations... without any of the many things a manager needs to do in order to ensure that the work is getting done, clients are delighted, and relationships are both consistently positive and widening.

It was a bit of a mess. Not a disaster, just like a bunch of yarn on the floor that had been kicked around some. Not a tight ship. And we had some pretty big clients to keep happy.

I liked to run a tight ship. Not that I micro-managed, but I liked to have systems, procedures and controls, most of which were there to train, develop and save people from getting into hot water. Tools—to make it that if they needed help, they knew what to do and who to lean on. And process—so that I could actually run the business, rather than be forced to slowly feel my way as though a blind man in a dark alley who is always waiting to end up touching a rat in the shadows.

My first major client responsibility was with a large and international consumer packaged goods company who had more insights people per sales dollar than any other company in the world. They ran a tight ship. And we, in turn, were expected to be technically perfect, each time, across all their eight lines of business. That seems reasonable, right?

The trouble was, this was being run day to day by over-confident Shelley. With no oversight. And some things had been perhaps misinterpreted by clients and without any back-up, Shelley was not picking up on these misconceptions. She was a nice, smart and conscientious person, but she had no backup training at all from management. Like an ill-balanced travel trailer going down the highway at cruising speed, the oscillations just got bigger and bigger until it threatened to take us all off the roadway in a fiery ball of death.

I had to reassert control. That took some effort. And a few hurt feelings. Retraining on my part, then reeducation and tapdancing with the client teams, and finally assurances that this would not repeat, ever. But we righted that ship and kept going. We all learned a lot and were better for it in the end.

The next client experience was more to my liking: video-gaming. We were working with one of the leading publishers of video games, testing their ads to make sure they resonated with the largely teenage audience. Trouble was, my day-to-day on this was Staci, a 35-year-old conservative woman from middle America. A very honest, pleasant and polite person, she was a technically excellent and self-aware researcher. But not to her fault, she had much trouble relating to the ads, the product and the marketplace. Our first ad was for a skateboarding game. That went well and I helped her with that. The next was for a "gangsta" type open-world, car chase/drug dealing/crime game. When she presented the results in LA to the marketing and creative teams, she had to use the word 'gangsta' and the very idea of this suburban "soccer mom" type person using the word "gangsta," well everyone just busted a gut. And I mean everyone – first of all Staci. We all appreciated the irony, and went all in. It added to the fun. She was a great person and we could not have accomplished what we did without her sizable contributions to the team.

Later that day Staci and I had another results presentation on another side of LA to another big client of ours: a skin care products company that marketed almost exclusively to women. I still remember sitting at that table as Staci presented. All women. All in their 20s and 30s. All fashionistas. Talking about various womens' products. I felt about as out of water here as Staci had at the video game meeting earlier that day. I was never so worried about relating to a consumer in my career as in this moment.

But one can learn anything, and in time, thanks to Staci, and to a few very patient people on the client side, I learned the business. Together, we developed one of the tightest ad testing programs ever, each ad building knowledge, and often to incrementally better in-market results. Their general manager used to come to all our presentations, and complimented us on how our work helped him really truly understand things. And this brand? It was one of the most successful in this Fortune 50 company.

Video gaming became a comfort zone for our team, and we worked to advertise many of the biggest video game franchises in the business today. While I loved this, I have to admit that some video gaming companies are just nuts: Many firms (not all) work like perennial startups, spend like reckless drunken sailors and while they might use insights, in those days they tended to only follow recommendations selectively – and ignored things that did not agree with their instincts.

I remember one project in particular that we did for a big video gaming client. These were always short-fuse projects with presentations that were days or sometimes only hours away from product launch. This necessitated doing a lot of work, and even presentation, while on the road. In this particular project, the game was a first-person shooter game. The ad we had tested involved a 30-second movie of sorts: a special forces team breaching a compound in a distant land, in order to get the bad guys. One tactic we used was to bring the arc of the "mini-movie" to a crescendo and then feature a potent gaming critic's accolade about the game, right before showing the logo. What I told the team was this: "Timing is everything. We need to generate even more attention here, and the best thing to do is to use C-4 to make a huge noise, just like before, and use those explosions to really get peoples' attention before the end." The people on the call scribbled notes and took that suggestion to make the ad even stronger. That was my typical value-add, and I smiled at the conclusion of the call.

Getting off the phone, I looked around to see many pale, slack-jawed, shocked faces of people around me. I had forgotten: I was sitting at a crowded boarding gate at LAX, and we were all about to get on a plane to San Francisco. I muttered some feeble excuse about advertising, it's not real... and "I'm so sorry." I am still amazed that I was not tasered, cuffed and processed that afternoon. But I never made that mistake again!

My favorite video gaming client was Nintendo. They were focused and wonderful. Nintendo of America tested everything, and acted on almost every finding. Immediately. Video gaming is an odd category. Some games are better than others. And when a game was bad (and reviewed by critics as bad), no amount of adjustment to advertising made any difference. Sales would not go anywhere. But when a game was good, ads had some "runway" and in this sort of situation, ad research typically helped to make the ads even more attention-getting and powerful. Seeing this, Nintendo believed in marketing research. The president of the company sat in on each and every presentation, either in person or by video link. The CMO became a champion of ours once he saw that our approach was helping his campaigns. And, unlike many presentations where results are presented and then actions are agreed upon days later, at Nintendo the actions were debated openly and fairly and actions were agreed upon right there, in the meeting. Then, on they went! It was a truly great organization and a wonderful collaboration.

A bias toward action. Nintendo was not alone in this approach. Other notable clients who believed in that approach included Levi Strauss & Co. and Amazon to mention just a few other favorites. They employed extremely smart people who prepared thoroughly, listened intently, and made sure that all decision makers were actually in the room. They discussed the findings, recommendations and implications of everything we had presented both politely and respectfully. Then as a group they made decisions and moved on.

One of the things that jarred me as we started to work with Amazon was the Jeff Bezos directive about PowerPoint. He hated it. PowerPoint might be tolerated when a supplier came initially to talk about capabilities or even meta-learnings, but it was strictly forbidden when presenting their research results. I had learned that Bezos was of the opinion that you needed to be able to concisely put the key findings into a few paragraphs on a piece of paper. Perhaps a table or two of numbers would also enhance understanding. But no charts and graphs, flowcharts or other visual doilies.

Being used to working with PowerPoint for many years and even using PowerPoint as a way to flow through my thinking about a set of data, I was at first rankled by this "No PowerPoint" dictate, but in the end, I will admit that it proved to be an efficient way to work, given Amazon's unique and disciplined culture at the time.

Bezos was big on 100% preparation, and no-excuses for failing to participate. He insisted that everyone read the one- or two-page pre-read thoroughly, thoughtfully and well before the meeting so that they might reflect on it. Then, like several other clients, they came, and we all discussed, listened, learned and acted immediately. They believed in research, and I believed in them.

A POET'S LEGACY ON A RAZOR'S EDGE

MOTORHEAD

Flat out: Me and my team developed the automotive ad testing practice at Ipsos-ASI. At the time I had a brand-new employee who I'll call Janie, who worked in the Eastern Time Zone. Together, we ended up testing perhaps 300 automotive ads for a variety of brands. She rose through the ranks and ended up becoming our sector advertising expert across Ipsos.

We grew this business incrementally. It started when we were approached by Ford in about 2006. When I caught wind of this, I jumped in and volunteered to lead the charge, arguing that while we did not have any automotive experience, I had scads of experience in both advertising as well as branding work (from my Saturn days). My bosses agreed.

It was quite the long shot and as a trial from Ford, we were given four ads to test. They had tested their effectiveness with another firm, and so were judging us in comparison, by our process and analysis. Knowing this, I did personally all the analysis and pulled out all the stops. I then edited obsessively for about 36 hours with only a few short breaks to sleep. It was fanatical but proportionate to the opportunity that I saw, given that a) we had no car clients, b) car advertising was the #1 biggest volume potential in the advertising production world and c) the more ads that are produced, the greater the need to test them for effectiveness. Net net, it had absolutely huge sales and strategic business development potential for Ipsos-ASI.

They loved our work: what we had to say and how we said it. We won hands down. After the first presentation, they asked us to stay the afternoon and to come back after lunch and so that we could present again, this time to the marketing team. So we did. After we concluded our presentation, they asked us to leave the room. Then, they came back after a bit and asked us to present it one last time to their boss's boss. After that third presentation I was remembering The Captain's order of "clients come first." We were all looking at our watches, hoping there were late flights out, when the bosses boss came in. She smiled, extended her hand, looked me in the eye and said, "If this all works as planned, we are going to keep you very busy for a very long time."

We almost lost this account merely a month later. We had been asked to test a series of ads for one of their brands, and when the results came back, all ads did horribly. To make matters worse, I was lined up to present the results to the head of this brand group and all of his team – about 20 people in total.

When I presented, I tended to start with an overview, and then get into the nitty gritty, finishing up with our recommendations for next steps. As I began my overview, the head of this group (a fellow that by his actions seemed like he never suffered anyone, and only talked to God) stopped me in mid-sentence, stood up at the head of the large table.

This EVP of whatever the hell Division then exclaimed, "So...(long pause) Roger! What should I do, just go out and shoot myself now?!?"

The reader may remember that first, my damn name is Rod, not Roger. Second, that I really hate bullies. The reader may also remember that I used to be in a damn gang, and knew how to fight. But the reader can take a breath because even though I wanted to punch this guy to hell and back, I contained myself.

I kept my composure and smiled, probably an epically fakey smile, but a smile nonetheless. I flipped to the reco slides and said, "well, lucky for you, (insert his actual name), you can put your gun away for today." And then I read off the things they could do to rescue his shitty series of ads.

Somehow, we got through this and retained the account. I am sure my friend at Ford needed a good stiff drink that evening.

Ford became a huge client and we developed a deep and meaningful relationship with our clients which lasted for several wonderful years. In the end, like many such relationships, it changed as a direct effect of up-top changes in marketing leadership at Ford. The philosophy to test or not is like deciding whether to go to church or not. There's no telling, no convincing, no debate. Suddenly we had a guy in charge who hated testing. Period. It was unfortunately, the end.

But the nice thing in all of this is that through becoming an automotive testing team, we used this to spider out. By the time our relationship with Ford came to its cliff-edge moment, we had a very sizeable normative database of automotive ads across about six different brands in the United States.

About a year later, General Motors called. And due to the Ford experience, we had a great (client-blind) story to tell, of course.

The pitch for this business was as intense as that for Ford, perhaps more so in that there were other political struggles that I had to face internally to make sure I could do it my way (with a small squad of experts per the approach I used at McDonalds). It was a hard-fought battle, but I got my way.

Two days before the upcoming General Motors presentation, the SF office (which I was not yet leading) hosted an Ipsos leadership cocktail hour at the Top of the Mark (Hopkins) in SF.

It was a glitzy affair. At that cocktail hour, the leader of Ipsos North America approached, and cordially asked about the upcoming pitch. We chatted briefly and in closing he wished me good luck. I smiled and in the presence of other global leaders said, "Thanks, but I do not believe in luck. I believe in hard work and expertise, and we have more of that than any other firm. We will absolutely win this. Thanks for your encouragement."

People were a bit taken aback; frankly I was not all that well known outside the US, and very few of them had any idea of who I was. I suppose I came off as a bit brash and confrontational. But in just a few days, we won the General Motors account, and I had a another, great metaphorical GM trophy.

But as any soldier knows there is winning the war, and then winning the peace. Winning the peace was not an easy task.

The steering committee overseeing this new ad testing effort at GM consisted of six people – half from the manufacturer, half from the agency side. It was a refreshing change having the agency people involved up front, and in the process of winning this account we and the agency people, together with the GM folks, had formed a great and lasting partnership. But we got off to a really strange start.

When we won this account, we spent *more than one month* developing a 100% consistent PowerPoint template for all copy testing reports. Really. One solid month. I know what your first reaction to this might be. Frankly, it was probably like my own, "what the hell are we doing?"

I really liked these people, each of them, individually but I could not understand for the life of me why we were burning so many hours on what I thought at the time was trivial nonsense.

We spent hour upon hour locked in a windowless room... all of us smart, expensive people. It was shocking! We took the "typical" report and put each slide up on the wall, then proceeded to pick apart each and every slide, one by one. This took days. Then we shuffled and reshuffled the deck over and over again. To get the sequence foolproof. Seriously. I thought I would have a panic attack!

Each and every slide, each and every section and even each and every phrase was designed to make misinterpretation or even willful bending of the data impossible. This procedure "fool-proofed" all the marketing research output.

We micro-managed each slide as to what would be on the slide, the typefaces used, the font sizes for headings, subheadings, copy and annotations. *Everything* was debated. The headings and subheadings themselves – *what* they would be called, *how* they would be indented. The *colors* used for stat testing, the benchmarks used for flagging differences, the terms for significance and directional differences. The order of the measures and metrics, of course. And the things that would and would not be in the appendices. It was a thorough, and occasionally mind-numbing exercise. The slides-per-hour speed was about four. Four slides per hour. I am dead serious. And then we'd debate if we even needed that slide. If there had been a window, I might have leapt out of it!

GM's extremely standardized method, with routinized metrics and even words used to describe findings insured that people could pick up *any* report from *anywhere* in the world and compare any ad with any other ad with total clarity and consistency. It worked.

With General Motors it turns out that the reporting needs were quite demanding because the intel reporting dynamics were all about total control of data interpretation, even in the most decentralized circumstances. In designing each slide, we had to "red team" it to ensure that there was no possible way to misinterpret the data.

In time I easily saw through example why this was so critically important to their mission. *I was the most surprised of anyone as to my total change of heart and opinion.* The reason lay in how General Motors tests, and in the power which carefully designed consistency and control have on making sure that things get done right, and not misinterpreted or misused.

I had to see it in order to "get it." It turned out that as soon as a report was disseminated, people were prone (as they are in may organizations) to totally misinterpreting the results. But because we had agonized over our reporting template, and had "fool-proofed" each slide even if it was taken totally out of context, this tendency to misinterpretation or even willful misuse was minimized and in time, virtually eliminated.

I cannot help but think that this careful consistency and control in some respects, paralleled the way in which GM manufactured and supported car sales worldwide.

This approach is also worth a sidebar discussion in light of McDonald's operating manuals, referenced earlier in this book.

On the McDonalds' business back in Spokane, I had been very taken with the extreme minutiae in their franchisee operational manuals. The way in which a Sausage McMuffin with Egg (or SME) is made in France, for example, is exactly the same way it is built in Fresno, California. And so it goes. Consistency and control. And when you are managing a worldwide brand, this all makes so much sense! It is absolutely imperative that everything be the same... and 100% always on brand. This is, of course, especially true with food, and with the human factor in serving and supporting food. So it was with McDonalds that every nuance of how the product/building is run had been brilliantly overthought, in the service of protecting the brand.

Other food franchises have less control, less uniformity and that leaves the whole equation open to consumer surprise ... not always a good thing when trying to manage a brand. I tell you this, if ever I am in a sketchy place and worry about sanitation, I eat at McDonalds. I know what I am getting there, every time.

The General Motors relationship became one of the best and most collaborative of client situations I enjoyed while at Ipsos – and that is saying a lot. The team and people we interfaced with were quite on their game, and we all developed a mutual respect for, and trust in one another. Through that process our team did some really good work and helped develop a strongly effective advertising program.

MESSY HUMANS: A SOCIAL EXPERIMENT

One of the most rewarding, challenging and subtle chapters of my career came in the last ten years: people management.

But I made a lot of mistakes on my way to this point. While I had management responsibility early on, I had absolutely no training in managing people or processes, and sometimes would inadvertently make a royal mess of things. But as I gained experience, I got better. So, I have to apologize for any crap I put people through as I became a better manager and human being. The last ten were my best.

At Ipsos, while I had direct managerial responsibility for about 25 professionals, the greater Ipsos office headcount ranged from 35 to (later) over 90 people. During this period, Ipsos had wisely decreed that each office would have one person as its leader. That person, through the last decade or so, was me.

I tried to focus around a few principles during my time there:

1/ we all learn from one another, regardless of experience, stature, rank, title.

2/ we all depend upon one another for support, help, service, experience.

3/ growth is key. We should all work for this. Why? Growth creates more pay, better opportunities for each person and bigger budgets for group fun (I made sure we had a lot of that).

4/ I do not care about what time you are here, or what time you leave. Just get it done.

5/ if you need help, your job is to ask for help. Do your job.

6/ no burritos in the damn dishwasher. Seems obvious, but no. Somebody once did that and broke it hard. In other words, act responsibly, respect your co-workers. Don't be a dick.

I posted this on the bulletin board or in places that had conspicuous position. I found that this was as close as we might come to our foundational document: our constitution, or our bill of rights. I made sure to remind people of these things again and again, over and over, and in time, this actually became the structure of our culture. This repetition was necessary, not only so as to make sure newer employees were on the program, but also to ensure that everyone knew that these thoughts were not "just some words somebody said." They meant something. Again, this became our culture, separate and apart from that of the parent company, Ipsos. And I never got any flack for that.

I had always respected the social experiment that was Landor Associates. In that situation, Walter and his friends had carefully hand-picked people like one might do in selecting attendees for a dinner party: people who would complement one another and taken as a whole, would be a marvelous mix of people, cultures and capabilities.

This was my chance to do something great. Something real. Something that would lift them up. I tried to architect that within my team and beyond, within our office. In service of this mission, I tended to be frustratingly selective in my hire decisions. Some colleagues did not understand what I was trying to do and could not imagine why I would be so picky and then hire one person over another, when the evidence suggested that the latter person might be technically more qualified. I selected people knowing full well that wrong hires could make for a toxic situation. I was as careful as a cook in making sure that none of the spices overpowered the others.

I made no secret of how selective we were. This too helped us develop and foster a high morale, a sense of pride and dignity.

In our marvelous mélange, everyone had a super power. I championed this actively. Everyone learned from one another (as I had said before). It was very "three musketeers:" all for one and one for all. Helping each other was the primary goal, always. The opposite of sabotage; it was mutual support and assistance. I made sure that if someone was really good at a thing, they became the designated experts and teachers. I gave them venues to help others learn, I applauded generosity of spirit and knowledge. And I reminded them again and again of our values and shared commitment to one another. Everyone who was here was special; that's why they got hired. And we had front row center seats to the biggest and grandest technology rise in the history of our civilization. We were all lucky beyond measure.

I used positive messaging, positive reinforcement and avoided negative threats as much as possible. To be sure, there were a few times that I had to get tough and insist on things vis-à-vis process or procedure. Mostly such things were about housekeeping issues and respecting one's peers (sharing in the chores, keeping a tidy work space, respecting peoples' space, etc.) but they were the rare exceptions. And when people were let go (and a few were, of course), it was done with dignity and respect for the individuals involved.

We had fun. We had great times. My team would party on and on together; they genuinely enjoyed one another's company, and this made me smile brighter than they could ever imagine. It was a real, true team.

Esprit de corps was higher than any place I have ever worked. When people left, we celebrated them. When people had birthdays, we celebrated them. When we got new accounts, we celebrated them. Lots of celebration made for a lot of friendships, and good and relaxed times.

Whenever a person left, I made sure we threw them a party. Sometimes I paid for it myself. Even if I hated that they were leaving, and putting us in a bad place... I celebrated them. I did this for them, gave them the best sendoff that I could manage, and made sure that we all celebrated their contribution to the team. This helped everyone, of course. It all comes back to you in the end.

Sometimes nothing –accounts, new business, staff conflicts – was as important as finding opportunity for shared food and celebration. Chocolate, pizza, cookies on those days when everyone was grinding as hard as they could and needed a damn break. No matter the day or situation, I tried to make sure that everyone felt good, positive, valued, and most of all just plain happy.

I personally bought and assembled a 300-pound professional foosball table for our team, and fought our HR department in order to get it in and keep it front and center. While only used occasionally, it had an outsized role, as sort of our statue of liberty at one point. A thumb in the eye of stuffiness and decorum. Much of Ipsos followed in our pioneering wake.

When we moved our office location, I fought fiercely to get them the most beautiful and visually rewarding workspace we could find: right on the waterfront of San Francisco. Our space looked out on the Ferry Building, Treasure Island, and the Bay Bridge. When it came time to develop seating charts, I gave the rank-and-file the best views: the very best seats in the house. I sat in the back. I had each person fill out a form telling me the two people they worked most often with, and the two people they hung out with. And I used that information iteratively to develop a seating scheme that made everything convenient and interpersonally comfortable for them. My people... they came first.

I listened closely to everyone. I watched for nonverbal behaviors and made slight adjustments to seating based on a few cultural and other interpersonal issues. Again, I did this to make sure that each and every person was comfortable.

That's the thing: care, comfort and relaxation. I know this might seem antithetical to the stress and pressure situations that many people have faced in their professional lives, and to be sure, we had clients who brought a lot of stress and pressure. But that's the difference: we were there to aid, abet and support one another through the tough moments, tough deadlines, impossible demands. And in that, we had higher satisfaction, lower employee turnover and consistently high-quality work product. It cost each of us very little, and paid each of us much.

LEAVING ALL THAT'S LEFT

There is a time to leave your stool at the bar and head for the door, to make room for someone else.

Several times during my life I had miserably failed to listen to that part of me. I missed my opportunity. I stayed too long. I drank too deeply and did not look out for the longer term. And by the time I left some of these situations, I realized that I had both overstayed and overplayed a once good hand.

This time was different.

Being the leader of the San Francisco office of Ipsos was wonderful but also certainly had its challenges. A few people within the wider organization were absolute thorns in my side. And a few were just innocuous obstacles. Unfortunately, and candidly, a few were out and out enemies. Of this last group, I can say that almost all of them got their just treatment – usually at the hands of others in the Universe. I am convinced that the Universe takes care of such people, eventually.

In one memorable instance, I was given the chance to watch the decline of an arch-enemy. If this person ever reads this passage, I am sure this person will know who they are. This last episode in my career was also one of the most memorable both for the situation and the character involved.

I have always had a pretty quick read on people, and after being introduced to this guy Vinny, for the first time right before a client meeting, I almost instantly knew to give him as much of a wide berth as I would a snake. Vinny proved to be a particularly malevolent and manipulative fellow.

Here's the guy: he had an inescapably criminal veneer about him, drove a Cadillac with tinted windows as if he had something to hide and needed fast getaway car. He reminded me a little bit of a distressingly anxious pit bull. He was always looking for personal advantage. And it was not just me who got the heebie-jeebies around him; most senior clients and chief marketing officers tended to avoid him, too. He just felt dangerous.

He met my expectations! In my short time knowing him, Vinny gradually acquired organizational control over things and groups that were far in excess of his abilities to master them. That was dangerous enough. To make matters worse for me, however, he seemed to do everything he could to box me and my team into a corner and minimize our contributions to the company. He stole my best hires. He took my clients. He bad-mouthed me to everyone he could talk to. He lied, cheated and stole from me and many in order to make himself look good and protect his ill-gotten turf. And he used his account empire to threaten and skate above it all. I mistakenly held my tongue on this, assuming that others would see through his façade and see the real "Eddy Haskell" character for what it was. But it was slow to come.

But the Universe catches up with people eventually. Finally, Vinny's nature caught up with him: he miscalculated during one of his self-aggrandizing maneuvers and messed with one of the company's leaders. He got caught red-handed and red-faced.

It was a career-killing mistake for Vinny. What made his ending all so memorable is that it all came to a head while about eight of us (including Vinny) were all at dinner one late evening with our laser-focused, quick witted and very intense leader, Paul.

Paul had, earlier that same day, discovered the latest of Vinny's tricks in which he tried to apparently end-run Paul. Understandably, Paul was angry at such a betrayal – angrier than I had ever seen him. At the conclusion of the dinner, Paul started in, chastising (even scolding) Vinny in our presence, that he should not have done this thing. Then, Paul proceeded to explain to Vinny how this was a terrible thing, that this behavior suggested devious things about Vinny's character that were harmful to the company and to our team, and got into the nitty gritty of Vinny's deeper shortcomings. Paul verbally whipped Vinny repeatedly and in front of us all, as we watched around the dinner table... in total silence.

This spectacle went on for more than an hour. All through this, we lieutenants sat in stony, expressionless stillness, bearing witness to this singularly brutal event. I even texted my wife during this to share the sheer unbelievability of the scene with someone who could relate to all its' complexities. It was unrelenting, and as close to an actual public flogging as I have ever witnessed. Vinny was hurt, beaten and sensing his impending doom.

Then, at one point near the conclusion of this flogging, he locked his tortured eyes with mine. Now, I was the only person at that table who had such a day-to-day understanding of the man in all his bizarre levels of complexity. The look in Vinny's eyes begged for rescue. And I had always loved a good rescue.

But given all that he had done to me, to my people, and to the firm, I looked inside myself and found my well of empathy completely empty. Bone dry. I had no feelings of mercy for this man, at all. I wanted justice. I wanted him to be scrubbed away. Erased. And at that moment, with the memories of all our horrible and unfair history with him, of unfair treatment and checkmate games he had played with me and my team, I simply met his eyes with a cold stare, and reminded myself that this was all self-inflicted, and Vinny's alone, to own forever.

I held his gaze and thought, "Live by the sword, die by the sword, you bastard." And in time, it was he who looked away.

About a week later it was announced that Vinny had left the company "to pursue other interests." A few days later, a smiling and upbeat Paul visited me in my San Francisco office, to make sure I knew the deed had been done, leaving me with no doubt as to the precise mechanism of Vinny's departure.

As I have said, others who messed with me got their just deserts. This last one, though, was the last, and the most vivid. Sometimes, seeing justice done can be both righteous and memorable.

Leading the San Francisco office felt great: I tried as much as possible to be everyone's protector and champion and, when feasible, to be their mentor. I genuinely cared about them, listened to them, accommodated their needs and generally tried my damnedest to give them a career experience which was second to none. *This was, I knew, my last time "at bat:" and I tried as hard as I could to be the boss that I had always wanted, and sometimes got.*

I came to a point, though, where the repetitive nature of the job – leading, cheerleading, getting new business, and then the bureaucratic process of arguing with others in the organization over and over about the same procedural things just became uninspiring and occasionally aggravating. As one fellow put it to me, "It is like having someone borrow your watch and then ask you what time it is." That is to say, after having gone to great lengths to educate people on what they need to do and know, they ignore everything you have ever done and said, and ask you anyway. Over and over. As if they had the inability to remember anything at all.

Sometimes this organizational amnesia and a repetitive tendency toward self-destruction drove me batty, especially over things like client chemistry, relationships and technology issues – each of these topics being things which really are not all that complicated at their core, but somehow became inordinately byzantine and opaque. In these moments I felt like I was trying to teach calculus to cats: never knowing how or where to begin, and feeling like it was a doomed quest from the start.

I suppose this happens in every organization; hell, I know it does. But I just plain ran out of patience. Patience, as God and my wife know too well, has never been my long suit, and this interpersonal type of agony is ultimately what pushed me out the door.

We kept going off the rails. It was like a death-wish. Time after time, big and strategic opportunities became mired in politically-motivated decisions which not only hurt our revenues, but also limited the contributions of gifted people. And I realized that because of the bureaucratic gordian knots within the organization, nothing I could ever do would change those complicated and emotionally-based dictums made by people with egos bigger than their brains.

In the Summer of 2019, my wife and I went on a backpacking trip, a pastime which we have held dear for all our 40 years together. At a campsite near a glacier in the Olympic Mountains, having walked through an amazing coastal rain forest, with open arms I exclaimed, "I could do this every day for the rest of my life."

My wife and life partner extraordinaire asked one deep question: "Are you still working at Ipsos for us, or are you doing this to prove something to yourself?"

Frankly, at one point, I *had* been doing this to prove something to myself. When I took this job in 2005, I told Ann that I wanted, as when I had been at Landor, to put my foot on the gas full throttle "to see how fast this damn thing can go." In about 2008, when the leaders of Ipsos came to the SF office during the height of the dot com bust that year, I told them "Stay the course, keep this office open. Tech will bounce back. Give it time. The SF office and its clients will form the basis of Ipsos' worldwide growth."

This all came to pass. Many of Ipsos largest customers were, at the time of my leaving, these SF-based firms. And I had been at least as involved as anyone in the full development of that result.

So, in the end, here I was: I did what I come to do. And now I was done.

The next morning, we set a retirement date. And stuck to it.

EPILOGUE

It was damn near perfect: they threw me a grand reception and dinner at my favorite restaurant in San Francisco. There were speeches. Some tears too.

I spoke briefly at my party, but avoided talking about my accomplishments in business at Ipsos or before. I talked, instead, about what I wanted them to *remember*: *to realize the importance of the people who believed in you, to note the lucky breaks you have been given, and the value of paying that forward: investing and mentoring your own people and teams in return... both the getting and the giving.* That was my last (and hopefully lasting) message. I hope this book has accomplished that task, too.

I felt both honored and special to have this final event with them all, knowing that few people get to enjoy such a thing these days.

On the next, and very last day of my employment, I turned in my Ipsos computer, and left San Francisco on the same ferryboat I had arrived on some 15 years prior. I walked to the fan tail for a last look and, while watching the city slowly recede against the fog, reflected on the fact that on the last work day of October, some 36 years previous, I had boarded a different ferry boat—the Klamath—to start a great adventure with Landor. Funny: boats have often played a role in my best adventures.

So, what great adventure comes next? Smiling at the mysteries of this wild arc of life, I itemized the great adventures yet to come. Standing at the stern of the ferryboat, I silently waved farewell, for now.

A POET'S LEGACY ON A RAZOR'S EDGE

"We shall not cease from exploration,

And the end of all our exploring

Will be to arrive at where we started,

And know the place for the first time."

– TS Elliot

ROD KELLER